WHO SAYS IT'S A WOMAN'S JOB TO CLEAN?

Library of Congress Cataloging in Publication Data

Aslett, Don, 1935-
   Who says it's a woman's job to clean?

      1. House cleaning. I. Title.
TX324.A7584   1986   648'.5
86-1617
ISBN 0-89879-215-0 (pbk.)

WHO SAYS IT'S A WOMAN'S JOB TO CLEAN?

By

Don Aslett

Illustrated by
Craig LaGory

Writer's
Digest
Books

Cincinnati, Ohio

Somewhere it started . . . that it's a woman's job to clean. It became a tradition . . . even an institution . . . and is still with us today.

Women are tired of it . . .

Some have gone on strike, refusing to deal with dirt or juggle junk any longer . . .

Some have stooped to devious means to get some cleaning help. . .

One woman shoveled all the family clutter into the swimming pool.

Another torched her house: "It seemed like the only way out."

Some have left for good . . .

And over the housework hassle, some have even resorted to the final direct approach.

The smell of burning brooms first drifted into the air during the late sixties. Most of us men ignored the chant of demands and shrank quietly out of sight, waiting for the calm of unquestioned house bondage to come back, for the rebellion to be over.

At the time, I saw all this as a sad waste of good cleaning equipment, because I was a struggling college student who depended on a broom to pay my way through school.

After thirty years now as a professional cleaner, writing four books and conducting hundreds of public appearances on the subject of cleaning, I've been called the "World's Number One Cleaning Expert." But "famous cleaner" or not, I'm sure that in attitude and performance you and I function about the same around the house. We men are so much alike it's almost uncanny. I try to tell my wife she got a better deal than other wives because I'm so dynamic, handsome, and in demand, and she tells me that I sound and act just like the rest of the males bouncing around the world.

The only difference is that from my exposure to the hundreds of thousands of women in my housecleaning seminars and the millions in my reading and viewing audiences, I've learned a few things that have finally caused me to surrender some of my male slobbism and snobbism and be a little more helpful around the house.

For years now, women have been trapped behind enemy lines. Lines of dishes, lines of dirty floors, lines of leaky faucets, lines of kids, lines of family excuses. Women are pinned down; they know the problem and they need performance, not sympathy.

I wrote this book because I wanted men to understand what women have been trying to say to them for years. I don't believe it's "HER" job to get others around the house to clean—through trickery, bribery, coaxing, or seduction. And I'm convinced that the only reason men are still dumping the housework on women is that they've never really thought about the unfairness of it all. I realize you were cheated out of the chance to clean—your mother never taught you—but I'm brash enough to believe I can teach you better than your mother ever could.

Your desire to be a better person, a fair person, a macho man, or a renowned gentleman will be immeasurably advanced by reading and using the material in the following pages. Every man has a secret mission to correct some social wrong. He yearns for the chance to make it right, whether it be helping an orphan or giving the starting place on the team to Casper TenThumbs. No wrong needs correction more than the unequal division of home chores and duties. Talk about a chance for glory and self-esteem! I promise you that nothing will be nobler than saving a woman from a dirty dish at the end of a discouraging day. *Try it—* you'll be amazed how much you like it.

P.S. You few who *do* do your share (or more) of housework: if your wife doesn't appreciate you, have *her* read this book!

Table of Contents

CHAPTER 1

How could a Man know anything about Cleaning?

Let me introduce myself before letting you in on what I've learned . . . about what it really means to be the man of the house.

When I was an energetic twenty-year-old, fresh off the farm and eager for a way to earn my way through college, a friend told me I should consider being a professional cleaner. "There isn't a woman in the world who doesn't need help with the housecleaning." "How do you do it?" I asked. "Just put an ad in the paper, and the women will call you."

And they did.

A Housecleaner is Born

Before I knew it, I found myself with a furnace-cleaning job, followed by some floors, then some windows. Next came wall washing and cupboard cleaning, carpet and upholstery care. On every job, the women would coach and direct me, and I would scrub, shovel, and polish.

Word got out that there was a husky housecleaner loose in the neighborhood, and soon I had more work than I could handle. I hired fellow students to help and taught them what the homemakers had taught me.

I didn't think much then about the demands on women for cleaning, because the harder it was for them to cope with it and the more they hated it, the better my business was. And the women chanted our praises as we diligently de-grimed their ceilings and uncluttered their closets.

In the next ten years, my housecleaning business received a good deal of notice—"COLLEGE BOY MAKES GOOD." Between newspaper headlines I acquired a lot of experience in housecleaning methodology. I ruined grand piano tops, pushed over china cabinets, broke windows, streaked walls, marred murals, shrank wall-to-wall carpets into throw rugs, and pulled scores of other goofs. But with each job I got better and faster and more efficient (at cleaning, not breaking!). I cleaned log cabins and plush mansions. I cleaned up after fires, floods, vandals, suicides, and after

husbands whose wives had been out of town for a few days. Some days I would have five crews going at once and my business grew steadily into a large professional organization cleaning houses, stores, banks, and factories.

By graduation time, I realized that I knew more about cleaning toilets than I did about dissecting frogs, so I decided to stay in the business. I snared off a few other graduates of pharmacy and psychology to manage my company and began to build it into what it is today, one of America's top cleaning firms. I got quite good at cleaning in the process, and you may have watched me on TV demonstrating professional cleaning methods. Or your wife may have attended one of my seminars and come home raving about how she learned to cut her cleaning time.

The reason I got to your wives is because my wife finally got to me. Seven years ago she announced that the theme for her church women's next mini-lesson was "The Art of Organized Cleaning." Would I give a presentation showing some professional secrets they could use in the home to save time and do a better job? As any of you would, I jumped at the chance to perform for a group of lovely ladies. I whittled out a little house for a visual aid, and taught a humorous one-hour session. After I finished I felt like Elvis Presley; they rushed me, ripped off my buttons, and begged for more material. Now when you've been a janitor and toilet cleaner for eighteen years and are suddenly mobbed by sixty women, you say to yourself, Man, this is living! So I did another and then another, each time adding a few more pro approaches and techniques and introducing the women to new professional tools. My audiences grew from 50 to 100, to 300 and then 900; my presentation stretched to three hours. I had a waiting list of people who wanted me to give seminars, from Seattle to Hartford to Miami. At every one, the women in my audience would sit hypnotized because someone was showing them how to cut that most dreaded and unrewarding word, HOUSEWORK, from their vocabulary.

This impressed me enough to sit down and write a book, *Is There Life After Housework?*

By November of 1982, *Is There Life After Housework?* made it to the bestseller list and for ten days was even ahead of *The Joy of Sex* and *30 Days to a Beautiful Bottom*. . . . One more hint that HOUSEWORK, overlooked and looked down on for centuries, was a hot subject.

A feature of the book that always brought shrieks of laughter from my audience was Chapter 5, "What to Expect out of Your Husband and Children"—after a handsome introductory illustration came nothing but blank pages. Although I did this—and even chose the title of the book itself—to let women know that I understood and sympathized with their problem, I gave them nothing more than a chuckle. I only paid lip service to the problem when you consider what I myself was still doing around our house. I sensed that my wife sure did a lot, and my heart went out to her, but my hands didn't go into the dishwater. Like most of our wives, mine got lots of appreciation and occasionally even roses, but still not much help.

True, like you maybe, I did the painting and repairing and the heavy work, but the food, clothes, floors, kids, etc.—90 percent of it was still, sad to say, the WOMAN'S job. I was providing a living—yet I still had the time to fish, hunt, play ball, or just goof off. I'd work late at the office, watch the news on TV, then stagger off to bed—leaving my boots, books, papers, popcorn hulls, and empty glass right where I finished.

Most of us think we do plenty, but in fact, on the average we are negative producers. We don't even clean up our own personal messes and projects, much less help out with the messes caused by others.

A Housecleaner is Reborn

Since she's married to a well-known and successful cleaning professional, you can imagine what the first and most frequently asked question is of my wife Barbara. You guessed it: "Does he do the cleaning at home?" And you can bet that the more times she's asked this the more conscious I become of what I do (and don't do) at home. After all, I know how, why, when, and what to do in every area of cleaning and I even write books about it. The truth is, I still have to kick and nudge and prod myself to keep myself aware of my output in the housework department. There *are* some tough habits to overcome here. For decades, hundreds, even thousands of years, housework was magically performed for us. We just had to get up from the table and presto, all the dirty dishes were soon clean, stacked in the cupboard. We only had to cast our dirty clothes in a hamper (or a pile) and zip, they reappeared clean and pressed and neatly hanging in the closet. If we noticed a spot or spill, we only had to twitch our nose or wrinkle our brow, ignore it ourselves a little longer and zap, it was gone! Some of us got so used to this female magic that we even expected the woman of the house to pay the bills without giving her enough money to do it.

My repentance really started when I began handing out "comment cards" in my seminars. The responses from the 180,000 women who attended were eye-opening, especially the answers to the question "Percentage of work done by spouse." Rich or poor, foreign or American-born, working or stay-at-homers, every woman filled it out the same: "0." Some would even cross out the "0" and mark "-10%." The comments were pleading, confused, pathetic—even aggressive—but they all said the same thing: "No one knows what is going on and no one helps."

For the first time in my life, I began to look at myself and what I saw wasn't very nice. I was one of the very people these women were complaining about. I would try on three shirts for my "big New York trip" and leave two on the bed. I was too lazy to clean up my own dishes after a meal when my wife was gone. I never turned my socks right side out. I didn't even know how to run the washer.

And whose example did my six children follow? Their father's, of course! School clothes, scout stuff, craft projects, curlers, toys, etc., were strewn all over our nice new home. You know the morning rush and scramble to get to work and school—after everyone's gone the woman walks into a room that looks like a hand grenade hit it. Two hours at the very beginning of the day wiped out—and for whose mess? Disgraceful, huh? Yet I, "The World's No. 1 Cleaning Expert," was doing it. I thought I was a nice guy and I loved my wife, but I deprived her of several hours of her day, every day, through carelessness and inconsideration.

I'd spent a lot of time in my professional speaking engagements trying to raise the self-esteem of professional cleaners. I know how put down and put upon they feel, even though they're doing a job that civilization couldn't do without. I'd even publicly bemoaned the fact that "the janitor" is often treated like a fixture. Then one day it dawned on me that the image of "cleaning"—in the world of professional cleaning and the home—is the same. People leave the building in the evening, leaving trash, ashes, debris, and dirtied, smeared, crumpled, rumpled things. Then the cleaners appear like phantoms in the night and by morning all is restored, ready to use and mess up again. It's the same at home—everyone takes all the positive for granted and notices only the negative.

The cleaning efforts of this world, at work and home, aren't just unrecognized and unappreciated. They're not shared and they're not respected. My professional (and now *home*) goal is to change that.

CHAPTER 2

What's been going on ?

I've seen a few books and articles that claim men are doing more housework. I guess 5 percent is better than nothing, but in truth men are not doing much more than they ever did.

Evidence

There are MEN vs. WOMEN studies, polls, predictions, analyses. They speculate and make assumptions and often contradict each other, but none of them give us any information we can't see for ourselves.

We don't need charts and certificates of proof—we see it and live it every day of the week. The evidence is before our eyes, everywhere. Ninety percent of housework is caused by men and children; 90 percent of cleaning up is done by women. We expect it, we allow it, we encourage it, and we seldom appreciate it. That's it—pure and simple!

For evidence, just look around: at family, relatives, neighbors. The woman is assigned to clean up after everyone, and the mess is always the woman's problem. She can be a real worker, a fast, efficient cleaner, and

personally immaculate but married to a mobile mud pie of a guy and the judgment on the resulting condition of the house, by everyone (even other unforgiving *women*) is "That woman's house looks terrible!"

Life today is different, more complicated than it's ever been. Many women are breadwinners and their time at home is limited. But even in situations where men are unemployed, looking for a job and hanging around the house, they can scarcely keep shaved and keep the beverage cans hauled out. Guess who comes home from work and does the cooking, cleaning, and domestic decision making . . . THE WOMAN!

Big healthy men go to school while the wife works, tends kids, cleans house, does the shopping and cooking; then the guy comes home sighing about how hard his day was and how exhausted he is.

The man has *his* dog and *his* car and *his* clothes until they are dirty, broken, or sick and suddenly they become *hers*. The wife takes the dog to the vet, does the laundry, runs to the dry cleaner, and arranges to get the car

fixed. Amazing transformation, huh?

At first I couldn't figure out the meaning of the squint-eyed look I usually got from the husband when I showed up to do a professional house-cleaning job. (After thirty years and cleaning thousands of homes I now understand the look perfectly—it was *guilt*!) Most of the work the women had me do could have been easily done by the man of the house, who often passed me on his way out to burn off some energy at the racquetball court.

I've carried box upon box from basements, walking right past sets of macho muscle-building equipment. I've torn out, then hauled off old fences and furnishings in homes where the husband owned a 4x4 pickup and had three days a week off. I've even been called by women to build shelves in carpenter's homes. In fact, in all these years I've very seldom done housework for women that they could have handled themselves—it was usually the heavy, the high, and the big-equipment jobs. After fifteen years of waiting for their husbands or sons to get around to it, the female decided hiring me was easier than nagging them.

The Shoemaker's Kids' Syndrome

*T*he fully certified automotive mechanic has had another successful day. In between routine brake jobs and carburetor rebuildings, he pulled off a beautiful salvage job on a car there weren't any replacement parts for, and managed to decipher the program on an unfamiliar vehicle's mini-computer. He comes home to discover that the stationwagon is stuck out on Route 17. It's the third time it's broken down this month, the third time he's given it a patch and a promise. Will he fix it right this time? —0—

A navy commissary officer served up exotic pastries and delicacies all through his stint in the service. He could feed an entire troopship smoothly and without strain because he was a marvel of quality and efficiency in the kitchen. Twenty years later, at home with his wife and family, he bakes and cooks: —0—

*T*he surgeon performs unsurpassed suturing every week. His delicate cuts and stitches are the salvation of the most difficult cases. At home a button pops off his dinner jacket. Does he sew it on? —0—

A noted landscaper grooms the grounds of the rich and famous daily, whistling happily all the while. He can design an herb garden or an orchard with ease and even the most finicky greenery thrives at the touch of his trowel. Will he help his wife plant the new rose bush in the backyard? —0—

*T*he award-winning chemist regularly writes up complex reports for prestigious technical journals. If he ever publishes his book he intends to thank his wife, who organizes all his research and does his manuscript typing. At home, does this brilliant man know how to brew coffee, operate a dryer, oven, or vacuum cleaner? —0—

A father takes his three boys to McDonald's for lunch and they eat a ton. When they're finished they all carefully clean up their mess—all the boxes, wrappers, paper cups and paper bags—and dump it all in the trash can. At supper that night at home they eat a ton. Do they carry their plates to the sink or put even one item in the trash? —0—

If every other occupation were added to this list, it would fill this book. Why won't we do these things at home? There's no logical or just excuse:

1. We know how
2. It needs to be done
3. It costs nothing for us to do it
4. We love our home
5. We have the time

It's not lack of pride or even laziness. Nothing speaks louder than action. There's only one reason: We *do* feel that—at home—IT'S A WOMAN'S JOB TO CLEAN.

Do Unto Your Own as You Do Unto Others

"My husband will work impossibly long hours for a friend, for a civic project, or for a political candidate, while the windows fall out of our house. He will cheerfully help out anyone else anywhere in the world."

Remember all those times your mother said to you: "You kids treat strangers better than you do your own brothers and sisters"—and we did. We do exactly the same thing in housework. While at another's place we will politely pick up our apple cores or break our necks to return the used lemonade glass to the sink, and always when getting up from a meal offer, "May I help?" Four hours later at home, we haven't the vaguest recollection of such action. That makes us downright hypocritical, and, worse than anything, do we hate being called a hypocrite. All the things we do at the homes of others and away—let's just try to do the same at home.

Ignorance, not Chauvinism

It's not necessarily chauvinism. Often it's ignorance. Cleaning awareness hardly exists for the average male. Very few men or children are aware of the housework that goes on all the time, right where they live.

I served as leader of a contingent of forty Boy Scouts for three national Jamborees, where more than 30,000 thirteen- to sixteen-year-olds travel to a mass camp for ten days of fun, experience, and education. These boys are the cream of the crop, as their rank and the qualifications to attend testify.

But it was like escorting forty flesh-covered garbage trucks. Every stop, every eating area, every motel room we left was a spoil of litter and waste. Ten scouts and their grown leader take a break and what do you find? Eleven pop cans! They can expand a single six-pack or snack package into twenty square feet of trash. On the ground under and around every outdoor table were mashed ketchup packets, half-eaten food, wrappers, silverware, openers, tools, and twisted, wrinkled books. I asked one bright-eyed fourteen-year-old: "Doesn't this mess bother you?" His answer: "I didn't notice it."

Boys' and leaders' tents alike looked like someone eggbeatered a Salvation Army store and dumped it a foot deep on the floor. Most would run completely out of socks, underwear, and money before giving a thought to replacement. Every burnt-out flashbulb, crumpled tissue, and pen out of ink was dropped, left, or laid right where it was finished with. And remember we're talking about *scouts* here—clean, healthy, honorable, well-disciplined, good family youth.

The toilet pumper at the last Jamboree said, "We've pumped shoes, belts, hats, pants, coats, shirts—you name it—out of these toilets." And it's not just kid stuff. Young men go off to college to learn how to manage a business when they can't even manage the aftermath of their own daily grooming. A colonel at a U.S. Army base told me, "Don, I have over twenty thousand people living here on base and almost none of them know how to clean when they get here. Someone has always done it for them at home, at school, and at work. They think floor stripper is the girl who dances at the local club."

It's Time for Equality of Vocabulary

I fumed and roared about ten years ago, when the equality thing hit my business and I had to go through everything and "de-sex" it—change the "man" in salesman, doorman, etc., and stop assuming, in my literature, that all managers were "he's." But the more I did it, the more logical it

seemed, and soon it even felt natural to think of a job as neutral in gender when in fact it was.

Now it occurs to me that we ought to finish the job and get the word "woman" out of the just-as-neutral roles of home and housework. "Hers" and "house" have become synonymous; home and housework terminology is so feminized it almost needs a Supreme Court ruling to abolish it. A scrubwoman is the woman who cleans a house; call a male a scrub man and it means he's too short to make the varsity team.

Consider:

Housewife

Cleaning lady

Charwoman

Mother's little helper

A woman's place is in the home

A woman's work is never done

"Her kitchen," "your cupboards," "your washer"

"Where do you keep the bleach, honey?"

"That's woman's work"

"Mom's home cooking"

"She can't cook, but I love her anyway"

"Honey, I'm home . . . Where's dinner?"

"Don't do the dishes tonight, sweetheart—I'll take you out to eat."

"Where'd you put my socks?"

"Honey, when you pack my clothes, be sure to bring my turquoise shorts."

"This place is always a mess!"

"Go ask your mother."

"Can't you get these kids to keep their rooms clean?"

"I bought you a new vacuum for your birthday, honey."

"I did your dishes for you."

Isn't it time we took the "y" out of "your"?

What's at the Bottom of All This? TRADITION!

It's going to take a while to cut the cords of tradition whereby the girls forever did the inside work and the boys did the outside work. WHY? Not one reason in the world other than it was handed down; mother did what her mother did, what her grandmother did, and what her great-grandmother did. Twenty years ago, forty years ago, it was traditional that women did the cleaning and men made the living for the household. Now many women are contributing financially to the family's support, and yet few men are doing housework. Men expect women to clean because their mothers did. Women feel guilty about not cleaning because their mothers did.

The TV ads aren't helping. Ever notice that it's always men who are making the appraisal of the clean shirts, the good food, etc.—but who is doing the work? Notice, too, it's always the daughter who went downtown and purchased the wrong cleaning product and the mother of much experience who tells her nay, a bargain is not necessarily a bargain. It's the daughter, not the son, we are still teaching to carry on the tradition. The male offspring is big enough to play little league and smart enough to run a computer, but he's allowed to spring into the house with grass-stained clothes and hand them to his mother. "Here, Mom, wash these!" Give me one—just ONE—good reason why it's a woman's job to clean any more than anyone else's.

It's easy to understand why we men automatically assume we'll be "cleaned up after." Mother and sister did it for us when we were babies (and beyond), janitors and teachers did it for us at school. The team manager cleaned our locker room, the city and county clean up the roads and parks after us and haul off our garbage. For a lifetime most of us have been taught that there will always be *someone* (generally a woman) to clean up after us.

We don't have to be intimidated by *tradition*. All it means is "the way they did things for a while." The way they did things then may not meet the needs of now. Today men and women do much the same kinds of work outside the home. It only makes sense that we share the same kinds of work *inside* the home, too.

A Day in the Life of a Housecleaner

My reputation as a "great clean-up expert" testified that I knew a lot about house*cleaning,* but, like most men, nothing about house*work.*

I still viewed, with a certain critical eye, the efforts of my wife and of other women as they struggled feverishly to get the housework accomplished. I ached to jump in and show those "disorganized gals" how an expert could square things away. The opportunity soon arrived. Early in our marriage I worked hard washing walls late at night to buy my wife a surprise plane ticket to Alaska. She was delighted to have her first flight ever and a chance to see her mother again. I bade her goodbye and told her to stay as long as she wished; I would take good care of our six small children. She wasted no time leaving, I assure you. My true thoughts were, "Now that I have her out of town, I'm going to shape up this house and make it as efficient as my business!"

I woke up at four the first morning and confidently mapped out the great campaign of household efficiency that was about to be launched in our home. By 6:30 A.M. the kids were up and they saluted before they went to the bathroom! By 7:30 the beds were made, the dishes were done, and I was rolling to victory.

We were putting the finishing touches on a new home, and my project for the day was the construction of a vanity cabinet in the master bathroom—an easy half-day's work. I had just started to glue the first board when *Waaa!* One of the kids had biffed another. I ran out, made peace, passed out the storybooks, and read a beautiful story. Then I picked up the board again. *Waaa!* Someone hurt a finger. Three Band-Aids and ten minutes of comforting and Mercurochrome-dabbing later, I picked up the hammer (after scraping off the now-dry glue) and had one nail started when *Waaa!*— a diaper to change (a cry which was repeated at intervals all day).

Again I returned to work and had started the second nail when *Ding-Dong,* the milkman. I slammed the cottage cheese in the refrigerator, then *Ding-Dong,* the mailman. I ran down and signed for a package, then *Ring-a-ling,* the school telephoning to ask about one of the kids' preschool registration. It's embarrassing enough when you don't know what a rubella shot is, but when you don't know your own kid's birthday, you're an outright scab! Then *Knock-knock,* "Can I borrow . . ." Then *Buzz*—time for lunch . . . time for bottles. *Waaa . . .!* diapers again, etc., etc. You wouldn't believe how my morning went. My building project looked like a chimpanzee special—dried glue and badly cut boards all over, and no real progress had *been* made.

Noon came and with it, another surprise. Those little dudes don't appreciate what you do for them, all that work cooking and they threw food, slobbered, and not one of them thanked me. I found out that to dress a kid once was just a warm-up. I re-clothed one of those kids four times by 1:15.

Nap time, and would you believe kids don't all go to sleep at the same time? I've bedded down 600 head of cattle more easily and quickly than those six kids. When I finally got them all down, no way was I going to hammer, play the stereo, or even turn a page loudly and risk waking them.

Fortunately, the day ended just before I did. I had two boards up on the cabinet by the time the last baby was ready to sleep. The most famous housecleaner and best organizer in the West had accomplished nothing. After that first day was over with—it was now midnight—I walked into our bedroom and shook and quivered like a man who's just received an IRS audit notice.

I'd never worked so hard in my life and I was right back where I started when I got up. I'd never had that feeling before. A woman lives with it every day. The week before three people asked me out for dinner, I bought four vans in one sweep of the hand, expanded my business into Arizona with a single phone call—but today I was just tired and discouraged.

I'll skip over the gory details of the next few days—but in general my "half-day" cabinet job, only half-complete, bit the dust. A week later my wife called to check on things. I pinched the kids to get them howling in the background so I wouldn't have to beg her to come and save me. She returned at once and I suddenly got efficient again.

Believe it or not, even wives who can devote full time to homemaking have normal days that are worse than our worst. In the "world" of work,

jobs are specialized and streamlined so that everyone can work efficiently: secretaries and receptionists answer the phone and otherwise run interference for managers; on a production line, tools and supplies are brought to the assemblers. The homemaker, however, does it all: answers the phone and the door, cleans, cooks, and does the wash, all the while minding an infant or a toddler and trying to slipcover the couch or paint the spare room. The "interruptions" in a homemaker's day can't be pushed off or "delegated": the first-grader who was teased on the playground has to be comforted, the neighbor organizing a block-watch program must be listened to, the friend who calls to discuss her problem child can't be ignored. But the homemaker still has to prepare those three meals that get eaten as soon as they're ready and clean that bathroom that immediately gets dirty again. And there's no supervisor to reward the homemaker with a raise or a promotion because she also found the time to teach her four-year-old to read or to grow organic vegetables in the garden.

We men really pull a cute trick when we, steeped in our business books, inform our wives that they must

learn to delegate. Now tell me, gentlemen, who can your wife delegate housework to? You are basically the *only* candidate, because if you don't do housework then for sure the kids (following Daddy's example) won't do any of it! There's no one in the business of housework to delegate to! But we men operate brilliantly at home by a process called Absentee Delegation, which means the body is absent when the works needs to be done!

An Ounce of Appreciation

Women are actually more embittered about lack of appreciation than about the dirty deal they get on the housework. They say the biggest problem is that when they are tired or overwhelmed by housework, it would be nice to get some understanding and encouragement rather than criticism.

Many women tell me that—unfair as it might be—they would ungrudgingly do all the housework if they received even an ounce of appreciation after it was done, or if someone just *noticed* it'd been done. One woman told me, "I don't care if he does it or not, just so he understands."

We men in casual conversation seem to say just the opposite, such as the friend of mine who in front of a group, graciously—even nobly—said "Dear, you go ahead and stay home [and take care of the house, yard, animals, and seven kids]. By darn, no wife of mine is going to work!" Another walked in from work at 5:30 and announced "Why don't you go ahead and run to PTA for an hour? I'll take care of your kids." Could you blame her for bristling to full blown and replying, "Mighty sweet of you to do that, since I tended them for you all day."?

All Hours are Equal

A confident husband pulled up in front of a specialty shop, parked his $33,000 Mercedes carefully, and strolled into the store. He paused to examine a new bread mixer, advertised to cut bread-making time dramatically. The clerk eased up to him and politely suggested, "Why don't you buy a bread mixer for your wife?" The man said triumphantly, "Why should I buy one? I *married* a bread mixer."

This kind of attitude is an incredible infringement of one person upon another. We men are undoubtedly the greatest offenders, because traditionally it's been taken for granted that a man's time is worth more than a woman's.

Although I thought I always treated my wife with consideration, I've found myself guilty of the same biases—assuming that her time wasn't worth as much as mine, sending her on errands, assigning her flunky projects because those time-consumers were an insult to someone of my capacity. A bread mixer, strangely enough, is what woke me up to the equality of hours.

I love homemade bread. Our entire family loves it. Whenever my wife baked bread, it disappeared with snorts and gobbles, without a thank-you, only the question, "When are you baking again?" Eighteen years of married life went by this way, the family prompting, begging, and scolding Mom when fresh bread wasn't available.

My wife never asked for a mixer; it was our teenagers who finally persuaded me to buy one. I put up quite a struggle since we were talking about $300 for "something for the house!" (I was spending more than that each year on football tickets for back-slapping salespeople I didn't even know.) When we finally got it, and I saw how fast and easy that little machine could whip out great bread, all I could think of was how much of my wife's time had been wasted—at least 2,000 hours—as she kneaded by hand for the past eighteen years.

It wasn't merely the cost of the mixer that postponed the purchase. Like most husbands, I would spend that much on a whim, under the guise of investment or charity. It was total insensitivity to the value of my wife's time. I'd simply assumed it was natural that a woman's time be taken up with mindless, repetitive tasks. My wife could have used those 2,000 hours for herself—to read or relax or play the piano or do something else she would have enjoyed more than pounding piles of dough. It's sad, but when most of us men get a mate to love and cherish for life, we figure that some extras come with her. She lives and loves, but she also cooks, sews, cleans, runs errands, and shops for us. We fully expect to pay for extra options on a car, but never in our wildest dreams do we expect to pay for the "extras"—work and attention beyond the call of duty—provided by a fellow human being: a woman. If a market value had ever been assigned to housework, and we were charged by the hour—few of us would be able to afford a relationship. Economists have estimated the actual value of the services that go into housework at $20,000 to $45,000 a year. But because it's never paid, it's never acknowledged.

All hours were created equal. Women's hours have sixty minutes in them, as do *ours*. Too many men think they married a bread mixer, a maid, a gardener, a taxi driver, a nurse, a washerwoman, an errand runner, forgetting that their mate is entitled to the same share of time as they are. For a human being, time is to love, to experience, to feel, to learn, to relax, to accomplish, or just to *be*. Position, occupation, status, age, and sex don't make any difference.

A FEW FACTS YOU MAY HAVE MISSED IN THE *WALL STREET JOURNAL*

● *A 1985 report evaluating a ten-year-long UN campaign to promote equality of the sexes found that women do two-thirds of the world's work, receive a tenth of its income, and own less than a hundredth of its property.*

● *From another UN study: The vast array of labor-saving devices in the modern world has not reduced the amount of housework; if anything, it has increased it.*

● *If the value of a wife's services in a home were included in the U.S. gross national income, that figure would double in a year.*

● *At least 52 percent of American women who are married also hold a job outside the home.*

● *A recent survey conducted by the* American Family Physician *reported that employed wives spend 26 hours a week on housework; their husbands spend 36 minutes a week.*

● *Another study indicates that women who are homemakers spend more than eight hours per day on house and family work, while women who are employed outside the home spend just under five hours a day.*

● *How happy do people report themselves to be? According to pollsters, married men are the happiest of all. Single women rank second, and even single working women with children rank higher on the happiness scale than married women with children. Married women rank third, and single men are at the very bottom of the happiness scale.*

Are You a Macho Man?

ARE YOU HOLDING UP YOUR END OF THE HOUSEWORK?
Find out with this test.

For each item, rate yourself. Circle your answer and transfer the number to the "Score" column, then add up all the numbers for your total score.

If you live in an apartment or condo-minium rather than a house (i.e., have no yardwork or maintenance to do), add 20 points to your score. If you have no children at home, add 15 points; no pets, add 2 points; no vehicle, add 8.

	Never	Once in a While	50% of the Time	Most of the Time	Always	Score
CLEANING						
I put my own stuff away	0	1	2	3	5	
I dispose of my old newspapers & maga-zines & junk mail	0	1	2	3	5	
I clean up my own project mess (sawdust, filings, dirty oil, etc.)	0	1	2	3	5	
I empty my own ashtrays	0	1	2	3	5	
I straighten up the house	0	1	2	3	5	
I dust	0	1	2	3	5	
I vacuum	0	1	2	3	5	
I sweep or mop the floors	0	1	2	3	5	

I clean the venetian blinds or take drapes to the cleaner	0	1	2	3	5
I wash the windows	0	1	2	3	5
I wash the walls	0	1	2	3	5
I clean the attic or the basement	0	1	2	3	5

BED

I make my own bed	0	1	2	3	5
I make the children's/guest's bed	0	1	2	3	5
I change the sheets	0	1	2	3	5

BATH

I hang my wet towel up after I shower or bathe	0	1	2	3	5
And wipe or squeegee down the shower walls or wipe out the tub	0	1	2	3	5
I clean my beard or mustache trimmings up out of the sink	0	1	2	3	5
I clean the toilet	0	1	2	3	5
I clean the bathroom	0	1	2	3	5

FOOD

I clean up after my between-meal snacks	0	1	2	3	5
I help plan meals	0	1	2	3	5
I shop for groceries and put them away	0	1	2	3	5
I cook meals	0	1	2	3	5
I set the table	0	1	2	3	5

	Never	Once in a While	50% of the Time	Most of the Time	Always	Score
I clear the table	0	1	2	3	5	
I do the dishes and put them away	0	1	2	3	5	
I help get ready for parties and get-togethers	0	1	2	3	5	
I clean out the refrigerator or defrost the freezer	0	1	2	3	5	

LAUNDRY

	Never	Once in a While	50% of the Time	Most of the Time	Always	Score
I hang up my clothes if they're still clean enough to wear	0	1	2	3	5	
I put my dirty clothes in the hamper	0	1	2	3	5	
I clean out my pockets and turn my socks and clothes right side out before I put them in the hamper	0	1	2	3	5	
I do the washing	0	1	2	3	5	
And drying	0	1	2	3	5	
I fold laundry and put it away	0	1	2	3	5	
I iron my own shirts	0	1	2	3	5	
I take clothes to the dry cleaner and pick them up	0	1	2	3	5	
I sew on buttons	0	1	2	3	5	

CHILDREN

	Never	Once in a While	50% of the Time	Most of the Time	Always	Score
I play with them and/or take them on outings	0	1	2	3	5	

I discipline them and referee disputes	0	1	2	3	5
I help out with their school projects	0	1	2	3	5
I take care of them or take them to the doctor when they're sick	0	1	2	3	5
I take them shopping for clothes	0	1	2	3	5
I change their diapers or help with potty detail	0	1	2	3	5
I feed them	0	1	2	3	5
I give them a bath	0	1	2	3	5
I dress them and help them find their shoes	0	1	2	3	5
I put them to bed	0	1	2	3	5
I chauffeur them to their activities	0	1	2	3	5
I arrange for a babysitter when we need one	0	1	2	3	5

GARBAGE

I take it out	0	1	2	3	5
I take it out without being asked	0	1	2	3	5
I take it to the curb on collection day	0	1	2	3	5

MAINTENANCE AND REPAIRS

I do the painting and papering	0	1	2	3	5
I fix/mend broken things around the house	0	1	2	3	5
I purchase the parts needed for household repairs	0	1	2	3	5
I arrange for repairs if I can't fix something	0	1	2	3	5
I replace lightbulbs and fuses	0	1	2	3	5

	Never	Once in a While	50% of the Time	Most of the Time	Always	Score
I tighten hinges, handles, and doorknobs as needed	0	1	2	3	5	
I catch and dispose of mice and insects	0	1	2	3	5	

OUTSIDE

	Never	Once in a While	50% of the Time	Most of the Time	Always	Score
I mow the lawn	0	1	2	3	5	
I water the lawn	0	1	2	3	5	
I rake the lawn	0	1	2	3	5	
I trim the yard (trees/shrubs)	0	1	2	3	5	
I care for our garden and/or flowerbeds	0	1	2	3	5	
I de-litter the grounds	0	1	2	3	5	
I shovel the walks/sweep and hose sidewalks	0	1	2	3	5	
I clean out the garage	0	1	2	3	5	

VEHICLES

	Never	Once in a While	50% of the Time	Most of the Time	Always	Score
I clean the inside of the car	0	1	2	3	5	
I wash the outside of the car	0	1	2	3	5	
I make sure the car has gas after I've used it	0	1	2	3	5	
I arrange for repairs	0	1	2	3	5	
I take the car to the repair shop	0	1	2	3	5	
I check and maintain oil, water, and other fluid levels	0	1	2	3	5	

MISCELLANEOUS

I run my own errands	0	1	2	3	5
I pack my own suitcases	0	1	2	3	5
I feed and clean up after my/our pets	0	1	2	3	5
I hire pro cleaning help when we need it	0	1	2	3	5
I make my own dental/medical/etc., appointments	0	1	2	3	5

Rate Yourself

Cad (0-25)	Underachiever (25-75)	Above Average (75-120)	Macho Man (120-160)	King Cleaner (160-390)
Egads, you cad! This book is probably your only hope of regaining the respect of the female species. Maybe you'd better read it twice.	*There's hope for you. Read the book before the end of the week. Once you apply what you've learned, you'll glow with self-esteem and other satisfactions . . . I PROMISE!*	*Nothing to brag about, but you're definitely above the average inconsiderate man. A careful study of these pages should bring you the rest of the way up to snuff.*	*Your example is invaluable. But do read all the way to the end to make sure there's nothing holding you back from absolute, total, amazing PERFECTION. And buy a copy as a gift for a worthless son-in-law or friend.*	*You're a liar! Go back and admit all the times you fudged the frequency of your contributions and adjust your score accordingly.*

CHAPTER 3

No more Feeble Excuses

We males do some of our most creative thinking when we're trying to weasel out of household chores. I know *you* wouldn't do it, but you probably have a friend or two who would be shameless enough to fall back on one or more of the following:

I haven't washed a dish in fifteen years

The guys would laugh at me (I'd never live it down)

No time! I've got tons of office work to do . . .

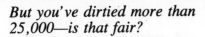

But you've dirtied more than 25,000—is that fair?

Would you ever live it down if your wife left you for a man who does dishes?

You didn't even have ounces of office work to do during the Wimbledon finals or the World Series.

It's a woman's job to clean . . .

Anyone using this oldest of all excuses is a feather short of a full headband. Anyone old enough to mess up is old enough to clean up—and that means both sexes.

I run things around my house

YES, you might try running things around the house for a change—things like the vacuum cleaner, the washer, the floor buffer, etc. . . .

My mother always . . .

She might be willing to take you back.

I have to be careful with my back/trick knee

It worked yesterday for racquetball and wrestling with the sons on the rug . . . not to mention co-ed aerobics class.

I'm allergic to oven cleaner

Playtex has more to offer than you imagined. (And you don't seem to have any problem with grease, oil, power-steering fluid, brake fluid, automatic-transmission fluid, or windshield washer concentrate.)

Only a sissy would clean . . .

Some might think it's sissy to wear designer cologne, flowered shirts, or to have your hair styled, but how could it be sissy to learn to be a rugged, responsible cleaning professional? An apron might be the sexiest piece of apparel you ever wore!

I already put in a hard week's work

That didn't stop you from driving to Louisville on Derby Day.

It's my day off . . .

Tell the diapers that.

With a degree in theoretical physics, you expect me to do manual labor?

Living is a hands-on profession, and the challenges of housework should be a cinch for a mind like yours.

The game is on . . .

Well, the soup isn't and won't be until the shopping's done!

I'll do it when I feel like it . . .

How do you feel when you wear dirty socks or a wrinkled shirt?

You're better at it

I bet you could give her some stiff competition if you tried.

Why can't the kids help?

They can, they just need an example to see how it's done.

It doesn't need doing yet

Haven't you heard? Preventive maintenance is in.

I wouldn't know where to start

A simple YES would be wonderful.

I don't know how . . .

Neither did she when she started. Now that you're admitting you need to know how to jump in and do it, read Chapter 6 of this book or pick up Is There Life After Housework? and you'll know more about cleaning than 50 percent of the people running around with a janitor's uniform on.

What do you think I married you for?

She's probably asking the same question.

I don't mind a mess

Is that why you keep making them?

It doesn't look bad

That's what you said right before the water heater exploded.

If I put it away, I won't be able to find it when I need it

Can you find it now?

If you didn't nag me all the time, I'd do it

She didn't nag you for the first ten years—and you never did it.

I'd just botch it up if I did it anyway

Only practice makes perfect.

I don't do _____

Good for you. But what if she said that about the cooking?

I do the outdoor work

Maybe you should move into the backyard.

Just leave it to me . . . I'll take care of it

"Leave it" is the key phrase here.

By now you can figure out the answer to the rest of these:

"You weren't gone long enough."

"I've got to help Stan move his stuffed sword-fish."

"You can't do that in this kind of weather." (It's too hot, too cold, too windy, too humid, too dry, it might rain, snow, sleet, or hail.)

"The [lawnmower, weed-eater, chain saw, drill, paint sprayer, etc.] needs work on it before I can do that."

"I have to take a nap first."

"I'll do it later."

"I'll do that on my vacation."

"I'll do it as soon as I get back."

CHAPTER 4

Yes we can!

The Fumbling Klutz Caper

It's masculine to be handy, but smarter to be unhandy. The "unhandy" man can escape all manner of make-it and fix-it jobs.

Women believe it, too! They've been brainwashed by all those cartoons showing the man of the house up to his neck in water trying to fix the plumbing, or some electrical engineer reading the Christmas toy assembly directions upside down. Or he studiously examines the broken or out-of-adjustment item and in a trial-lawyer voice says, "Mmmm . . . I don't have the right hex torch metric tool for this" or "we need a part from the Orkney Islands." Most women won't question tools or parts and the hunk of an unhandy husband slithers out of fixing things. And if all else fails, a despairing fling of the screwdriver will make any woman back off.

But there is absolutely no such thing as being unhandy at HOUSEWORK. Some men may have electrical, mechanical, or mathematical limitations, but there need be no housework hesitations. Anyone who can walk and chew gum at the same time can keep a home spotless. If you can wash your hands, you can wash anything. If you can polish a hubcap, you can polish a sink. And even if you can't pick off a sizzling grounder at first base you can pick up a shoe.

Hairy-Chested Housework

Would you believe that *elevation* even affects the housework we men are willing to do? Here is some scientific proof.

Somehow mountain air cures all housework apprehensions. We will sneaker-foot past simple housework duties at home, then lumber-foot into the forest and do every housework task in its most ghastly primitive state! We won't touch a dish, pan, package, or washing machine at home and we turn up our noses at a less-than-perfectly cooked egg. Yet hours later, in our rustic campsite, we will (fighting wind, ants, flies, or freezing temperatures) over a fire we had to hunt fuel for and build, reduce an innocent egg to a charred blob and happily eat it cold. We permanently blacken the virtue of spotless pans and kettles, while getting smoked, scorched, and greased-burned ourselves. We wash our clothes uncomplainingly by hand at a cold creekside and laboriously whisk out the tent with a pine branch. We even make

our bed fastidiously (roll up our sleeping bag and perform the gymnastics necessary to get it back into its stuff sack). And get this: we pack all these housework supplies on our backs so we can be *sure* to be able to perform it . . . and we even *pay* willingly and generously to get to do all this!

What could be more manly than

being fair and consistent? Home housework is not only ten times easier and more convenient to do, it's more impressive and appreciated than the most hairy-chested heroics. Be a real hero, carry your campfire consciousness back to the kitchen!

Military Maneuvers ...On the Home Front

I know for a fact those of you who've been in the armed forces know how to clean. You *had* to know, just to survive. You not only learned to cope with KP, to fit everything into a footlocker, and to keep everything in its place, but you even cleaned well enough to pass that dread WEEKLY INSPECTION. Your bed had to be made so taut a quarter would bounce off it; uniforms had to be knife-edge pressed; and you know well what it is to fall out of the barracks and police the area. Now that Uncle Sam isn't glaring down at you, you've simply slacked off. More likely than not, you're just out of the habit of doing things regularly and keeping things neat. Let's revive those spit and polish skills and use them on the home front! polish skills and use them on the home front!

We Can Do It . . . Because We DO Do It

Consider the fact that 80 percent of all the professional cleaning companies in the world are owned and operated by men, and of the cleaning chores they undertake to do, 70 percent are performed by men. Commercial cleaning is no different from the home type, except that commercial cleaning is actually harder—since it involves more square feet and heavier machinery.

Men Learn Faster!

Speaking as someone who's trained and employed tens of thousands of cleaning employees in homes and commercial establishments, I tell you that men catch on faster and work faster than women . . . even cleaning the delicate stuff! Once, for example, I was called to do a large job where a basement fire left a Canadian couple's home smoke-stained and damaged. You're not going to believe this, but they had (it was recorded on the insurance proof of loss) 7,200 individual figurines and shelved pieces of rare and unusual stuff.

Thinking like the average man, I figured this painstaking task was a

woman's job for sure, so I hired a group of women. They were slow—not as familiar with the mechanics of production, perhaps, as were my cleaning men, who were not only faster, but neater than their female counterparts.

We're Simply Better at It.

Most housework jobs are mechanical, and men are generally more at home with such chores than women. That's

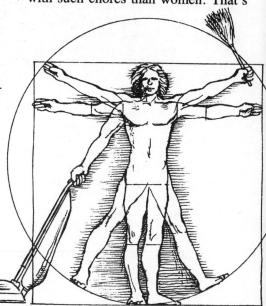

not just hearsay, it's a scientific fact. When you look at the nature of the operations involved in cleaning, and the equipment and supplies needed to do it—it's amazing that it was ever assigned to women in the first place.

Housework is tough, demanding, sometimes dangerous work that takes both skill and stamina.

As far as skill, no woman will ever be able to clean as well and as fast as a man. Men are more adept at manipulating objects (like mops and buckets), and they're taller, so they can reach high shelves in a single bound. They're stronger, so they can muscle those obstructions out of the way and lift and heave with ease. Their longer arms and strong hands can easily get the spot near the top, and they can climb more easily up the ladder to wash the ceiling or the walls. They excel at practical problem-solving, which housework abounds in, and are far less likely to spook at the sight of a spider or silverfish.

So you see, physically and emotionally, men are better suited to the basic requirements of cleaning (eat your heart out, you females). On the average, women are more meticulous and a little more consistent, but I believe this is not an inborn physical or

mental trait; simply the habit of commitment they have toward the job. As I and my crew of pro cleaners attacked hundreds of homes to clean them over the years, the women owners of the homes actually felt more confident when a male crew was working. Look around at who's cleaning our buildings and homes; women don't dominate the cleaning kingdom at work—why should they at home?

Your Share . . . Even Steven

There are many different time zones in the world. These are mostly very pre-

cise and accurate; only one is totally unpredictable and utterly erratic and that is the "last time" you did something!

We men think we help more than we do. Man after man (even ministers and scout leaders) will tell me in all sincerity and apparent honesty that

they help around the house. Yet not a one of them can tell me where the cleaning stuff is, or how to use it. Most can't get the new safety lids off, so that tells you something about when "the last time" was. Last times in cleaning are like when you last called a friend, went to the dentist, or had a physical. It wasn't days, weeks, or even months . . . but always *years* ago!

I read volumes and articles of theory and instruction about HOW and WHY to divide up the cleaning so everyone has his and her fair share. Get the word "share" out of your vocabulary. Thousands of words and little messages and lists have been written to get people to do their share of something. Splitting anything is always a risky business. No one—bank robbers, partners, commissioners, etc.—is at his best when it's time to divide the loot or the assignment.

In the housework arena, if you're worrying about each doing his or her exact share, forget it. We don't split work and *expect* each other to do his or her share—we both work together to get it done. If one finishes first, he helps the other so they can get it all done faster and do something else together. Everyone does all he or she can

in the time they can spare.

The cure to the "housework" problem will come from one basic thing: each of us being aware and considerate enough to take care of our own junk and mess, and being willing to pitch in once in a while behind someone else. It doesn't matter who did it last time; all that counts is that we end up with and enjoy a clean, neat setting—so just jump in and do it. DON'T KEEP SCORE!

And don't kid yourself. There's a big difference between *helping* and *doing*. For example, feeding the family—the never-ending job. A friend once said, "I take care of the food. I do the shopping."

Was he off! Taking care of the food means:

Planning the menu

Listing the ingredients needed

Picking them out (or finding them!) at the store

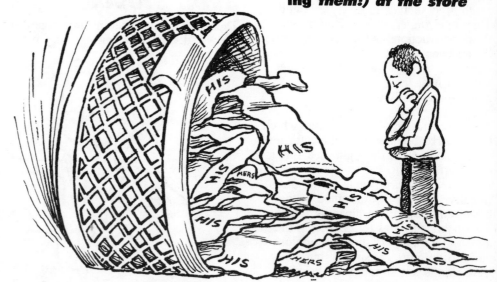

Bringing them home

Putting them away

Preparing them (washing, peeling, chopping, tenderizing, etc.)

Cooking

Setting and decorating the table

Serving the meal

Eating

Wiping up spills

Clearing the table

Cleaning the kitchen and eating area

Washing the dishes

Drying them

Putting them away

Canning and preserving

Planning and holding parties, etc.

The man of the house is often involved in only one of these steps—the eating. (Even when he goes to the store, he's not usually shopping, he's just following her list.) And though there are some men who cook, many others would only be caught with a basting brush in their hand at barbeques and other meals that involve an audience.

The same goes for laundry, of which some phase must be done every day:

Gathering dirty clothes from the hamper and elsewhere

Sorting

Pretreating stains

Washing

Drying

Folding

Ironing

Distributing

Mending as needed

Taking clothes to the dry cleaner and picking them up

Take the Initiative

A willingness to tackle something that needs to be done (without being asked or nagged) says appreciation. "Can I help you?" is better than nothing, but it doesn't express full love and commitment; taking the initiative does. My wife taught me a startling lesson in this regard. When friends of the family lost their father, I tried to express my compassion and concern by asking, "Is there anything I can do?" "Oh . . . no . . . there's not much anyone can do now." My wife, however, knew something we all need to learn and practice: don't ask, DO.

Barbara knew the whole family was coming from out of town to the home of the widow and things would be crowded. So she cleaned up our motor home, made up the beds, and drove the van over to their house and just left it there, so they couldn't refuse. Then she called and said, "The van is there, please use it." They loved it and they didn't have to ask.

We Can't Escape the Law of Carryover

It may be hard to imagine, but the personal value of cleaning is great. Getting someone to clean up our mess is about as smart as having them exercise, eat, and have sex for us. Cleaning our own messes keeps us in touch with things as they really are. If we only went to the party and didn't ever

The Woman's Night Out

help with the preparations or the clean-up, we'd never see the foundation of effort and organization that underlies even the most carefree moments. If we don't ever do laundry or mop a floor, we won't understand that restoration is a very real part of use.

Cleaning our own mess gets down into the heart of responsibility. What could be more basic than putting back in order the things we disordered, removing the dirt we ourselves tracked in?

Seventy percent of housework is clutter and litter control, and the daily demands of dealing with the aftermath of eating, grooming, dressing. It's the clothes we wear, the food and paper we go through daily. That's why housework isn't a woman's or even a family's job, but a personal, *individual* responsibility.

The biggest reason women shouldn't have to do all the cleaning is the unspoken implication of that. It's in effect saying: LET SOMEBODY ELSE DO IT!

Every pattern and attitude we acquire in one area of our life carries over into other areas. If we dodge our chores as a kid, we're likely to do the same in our marriage and our career. If we grow up wasting things, we may

well be wasteful of time and life later. The quitter on the kids' leaf raking team will probably be the quitter on the sales analysis team at work. People who never learned to see a mess around them won't recognize a problem when it happens in their business, health, or marriage.

If we learn at home (where we spend most of our time) to be unresponsive to commitments and promises, if we live at home insensitive to others' needs, we'll carry it right along with us to the outside world.

As I write this in a large scout camp dining hall, the head of the camp came in, plugged his razor in the socket on the center pole between tables, shaved with an electric razor, then took the razor head off and blew whiskers all over the tables and clean floor.

If we only did housework for one reason—the incalculable value of carryover—it would be worth it.

12 Reasons to Hog the Housework

1. Peace and a Clear Conscience

No more wasted time, no more mental anguish—dodging, sneaking, excuse-making, debating—no more nagging, bargaining, complaining, bitching, questioning, no more fights. Facing up to a few minutes of housework is much easier than haggling and scheming. Simply DOING some housework is the easy way out.

2. How Could You Reap Bigger Benefits from Just a Few Minutes a Day?

Doing your share plus a little extra will probably take about twenty minutes a day, maybe an hour or two on Saturday. Where can you find time for housework in your hectic schedule? What about the time you spend rereading the sports page, evaluating your neighbor's progress on his new sidewalk, or watching some idiot show on TV? Think for a minute—which will have the most dramatic effect on your life and home circumstances? It's an easy answer:
JUMP ON THE HOUSEWORK.

3. Exercise

Why waste your time riding stationary bicycles or wrestling on the floor with expensive muscle-building contraptions? Cleaning is the perfect exercise—just enough lifting, bending, and reaching to keep the old body in shape. Look around you (maybe even *at* you)—at all the men who are getting tank bellies and looking like waddling pears. Housework is exercise with a purpose, as well as a reward. Name any other exercise you can get (unless you're lucky enough to live on a farm) so conveniently.

4. Good Clean Therapy

Irritated, agitated, pent up, tense? Try a snort of housework. What a chance to unwind and put your body to work while your mind works out the frustrations (and maybe even the problem itself!). There's something about improving a dirty condition that also improves our mental condition; the act of cleaning has an oddly soothing and purifying effect. And as women have known for centuries, there's hardly a better or more productive way to work out guilt, anger, and aggravation.

5. You'll Get Real *Satisfaction* From It

After a day of shuffling papers and attending meetings, soldering circuits on the line, getting the runaround from the regional manager, or coping with the complaints of customers, you'll find the genuine *immediate* pleasure you get from looking at a freshly vacuumed floor or a newly washed window a refreshing change and a real thrill. You can see, feel, really *tell* what you did today. There's an undeniable satisfaction that comes with restoring order, with getting it all together. And dealing with things long overdue to be dealt with banishes guilt. In fact, the dirtier and messier things are, the better you'll feel when you're finished!

Besides, it's great to come from a difficult day to a clean home. All your senses have something to rejoice in, and the order that meets your eye when you open the door will fill you with a calm, restful feeling. You'll find immense satisfaction in knowing *you* created all this.

6. You'll Learn the Real Survival Skills of Modern Life

Forget those expensive courses in surviving desert disasters or Himalayan hardship. Unless you're rich, unemployed, or extraordinarily unlucky, you have about a 1-in-100,000 chance of ever putting them to use. But knowing how to take care of yourself in your everyday environment is a skill *nobody* should be without.

We all have to manage on our own sometime and these days we're all single longer—and more often. The man of the John Wayne generation who learns to clean won't ever have to marry just to have someone to keep house. And you men of the future *have* to know how to do it. The new crop of women growing up isn't going to do it all quietly, automatically, and uncomplainingly anymore. Besides, it'll make you more capable of attracting a dynamite mate.

7. At Last, You Can Have a Hand in Getting and Keeping Things the Way You Really Like Them

You're the one who wants the living room to always look presentable? Do you hate to see dishes left in the sink? And you *despise* the idea of somebody else messing with your stuff? Here's your big chance to "have it your way." You can help assure that your home is as clean, comfortable, and orderly as *YOU* want it to be and not just the way your mate happens to want things or is able to manage to keep things.

8. It's a Whole New Chance to Brag and Show Off

Forget that tired old talk of how many miles you ran or how you landed that monster trout. When you start reeling off those statistics of how many tile joints you whitened and toasters you shined, your buddies will be utterly speechless. This is a real growth area for one-upmanship.

9. You'll Save Money

Keeping things squared away keeps them from depreciating, rotting, breaking, getting stolen, rained on, etc. Carpet, drapes, furniture, all last longer if cleaned and maintained regularly—some things will last twice as long. Imagine replacing the rug every fifteen years instead of every six—that's a couple of thousand for a home computer or a VCR. You'll also save the use of professional cleaners; they cost money, and there's nothing they do that you can't; I promise you this is true!

10. Women Become Warm and Playful When . . .

The house is clean, squared away, and running smoothly. Take over some of the work and you'll have more time to play together. She'll be less irritated and naggy, prettier, a little more likely to believe that you really do *care* . . . and you can use your imagination from there. We'll really make all those macho foreign lovers sweat when we start making housework an all-American male passion.

11. A Chance to Give Good Example

Someone in the family, sometime, is going to have to break the tradition that it's the mother's and the daughters' job to clean, cook, wash, etc. Before you launch into the old trap of "share and assign" a regimented family cleaning program, remember that around the house EXAMPLE from the father is lots more effective than rules pasted on a bulletin board. You don't need to give stirring speeches; just the simple act of DOING some housework, without being asked, will do much more to change the lives of family members. Example is still the very best—if not the *only*—effective way to teach anything. It's the quickest, easiest, surest way to change attitudes and behavior patterns.

We men don't spend much time reaching and teaching our children; by doing the cleaning we are a living lesson plan going through the house. Housework is one of the few handy opportunities we have to gain our children's respect, show them how to be loving, thoughtful beings. Don't let it escape!

12. You Could Make a Career of It

(And you'll be trained for another profession when the depression comes).

I became a millionaire doing housework, and all the while I've been free and independent, kept in fine physical shape, and had the chance to travel the world and meet and enjoy tens of thousands of people. After you've learned to clean around the house and gotten your home in shape, you might want to think about doing it full or part time (or as a family) for a living.

You won't even have to clean under your fingernails; you can thumb your nose at all your high-pressure sales-pyramid relatives. And as you learn and grow, you'll want to find a way to do it faster and better like our brilliant species always does. You might even invent new tools and procedures and become rich and famous in the process.

CHAPTER 5

What can you do?

Ever step on a rake you forgot to pick up and get a punctured foot? Or have the handle zap you with a black eye? Ever find your pliers by sitting down on them, or back the car over something you laid down and left there? Ever need something in an emergency, and not be able to use it because you didn't put it back or fix it when you had it last?

These are just a few little examples of the kinds of problems we inflict upon ourselves through neglect and thoughtlessness. Imagine what these and similar habits do to *others* in our homes, offices, or organizations.

I heard this comment once and thought it summarized the situation well: a non-housecleaning husband said to his wife on Mother's Day, "Dear, is there any way that I can help you with the housework?" Her reply: "Dear, if you just clean up all of your own stuff there won't *be* any housework."

Examine your own conduct. It will be a revelation to you. Picking up and cleaning up after yourself will be the single most useful thing you can do. It's much more pleasant, easier, and safer to work in orderly surroundings. It took me a while but I finally discovered that if I put my wrenches away, my fishing stuff away, my baseball gear away, when it came time to work or play I could do it quick. I didn't have to hunt and rummage.

REMEMBER: There's nothing wrong with making a mess; that's often progress in the making. It's leaving it that is wrong. . . .

In short:

If you open it, close it

If you turn it on, turn it off

If you unlock it, lock it

If you break it, fix it

If you can't fix it, dump it

If you borrow it, return it

If you make a mess, clean it up

If you're done with it, put it back

If you don't know where it goes—ASK!

We Can be Our Own Buzzards!

I HATE IT WHEN HE LEAVES THE BIG STUFF.

When the West was being won, if a horse was injured or a wagon ruined, our rough, tough forebears shot the horse where it fell or shoved the wagon over a cliff—and moved on. Expired or exhausted things were tossed and left alongside the trail for the buzzards. We rugged males today are exactly the same. We can round up, find, prepare, and carry something fifty miles to use it, but we can't seem to make it fifty feet to get rid of it or put it away when we're done.

We seem especially incapable of disposing of anything empty (cans, bottles, jars, boxes). We finish it off, but almost *never* go any further. And when something quits working (mower, tiller, drill, etc.), isn't it amazing how the thing is instantly immobile? Machines, motors, even vehicles—we leave 'em right where they died. So we stumble over them as well as clutter up the place. It must be because we have a subconscious assurance that The Great Gatherer (a woman) will come by and pick it up for us.

Women shouldn't have to be our buzzards. If we're man enough to crush a can in one mighty squeeze, we ought to be able to toss it in the trash.

The Manly Art of Flinging

We males undoubtedly have an uncanny knack for "distributing" things.

My dad once asked me to pick up a "broadcaster" at the hardware store. I gave him a puzzled look and he said, "It's a machine you put stuff in, turn a handle, and it throws the stuff all over." Sound like a quick description of a man? The minute we turn the door handle of the house, we begin to "broadcast" things.

We start by tracking dirt in on our tractor-tire boots. We think being engrossed in an important project justifies not cleaning the grease off our hands. In fact, we're a little proud of it. Thus all we touch is marked; we even throw our oily coveralls on top of clean laundry! When (if) we do wash up, we leave the sink and everything else in the bathroom dirtier than we were. And guess who leaves those black heel marks on the clean kitchen floor?

We frown if a peeling is left on the counter, yet we always leave shavings, sawdust, filings, behind. We broadcast it all! The only time our gloves aren't flung somewhere is when we're wearing them. Most of us really believe the second purpose of socks and shoes is to test the agility of women's pick-up power. I'll bet that if there weren't women nurses cleaning up after male doctors, there would be livers, gizzards, and gallstones knee-deep in the surgery room!

In my nearly fifty years I've walked in the door after work as a manure-footed farmer, a grease-coated mechanic, a paint-spattered professional painter, a dusty sheetrock contractor, and a paper-scattering student. As I reflect on the reason for this thoughtlessness, I remember that even as a youth on the farm, the tracking in of straw or mud by men was tolerated because it was "work dirt." Who—especially a *woman*—would dare question the sanctity of work dirt? It was as hallowed as a battle scar!

The cause doesn't justify the mess! *Don't put it down—put it away!*

We know that a real man takes care of his own responsibilities. Our own daily personal mess should be Number 1. Who would be thoughtless enough to make another person clean up his leftovers and left-abouts? Not a MAN, I hope!

Here Are the Big Ten, Men . . .

1. CLOTHES CLUTTER: Your sole responsibility to clothes is not just wearing them, as has been supposed for at least 8,000 years. Caring for them—picking them up, hanging them up, folding them—cleaning and disposing of them when necessary are part of the picture, too. We value our clothes for comfort, image, looks—who should be more concerned with their maintenance, preservation, and accessibility than us!

2. FOOD MESS: The issue of dishes is covered in Chapter 6. The very *least* we can do is to not leave food container lids off, packages undone, food and drink empties and wrappers lying around (see opposite page).

3. PROJECT FALLOUT: Have we ever cleaned up after our wife or daughter's craft or school projects? NEVER! Have they ever cleaned up ours . . . ? The fact that we do a giant project doesn't give us immunity from the cleanup: sawdust, solder, wood chips, plaster dust, etc. We don't have to leave a mess in plain view to advertise our accomplishments. What we actually did accomplish will be appreciated

even *more* if it doesn't leave a giant cleanup job behind.

4. SPORTS MESS: We men play golf and shoot wild game and figure our activity is over when the day ends. We lay muddy boots and

shoes, bows and quivers, and racquets all over the living room and finally end up asking the wife what she is going to do with that smelly deer hide or those stiff unappetizing fish. Real sports put their sports stuff away after using it . . . and clean their own fish!

5. JUNK: Women are equally guilty of this, of course, but I'd like to note here that we men do have our

very own entirely masculine species of junk and clutter (which can be loosely defined as things we don't really want or need, but we keep around to clog our storage space, worry, and distract us). Raise your clutter consciousness today—see pp. 46-49—and put that tossing arm in action, brother!

6. DRAWER/CLOSET MESS: These are storage places, not directions to sling things in or hidden clutter bins. Keep drawers closed and neat.

7. PAPER CLUTTER: Magazines, newspapers, junk mail, and other mail is shamelessly piled and accumulated by the majority of us men, waiting for the woman or the maid to heave it. How are they supposed to know whether it's important, whether we're through with it or not, what we want to save, etc.? Let's take care of ALL our own paper products.

8. SMOKING RESIDUE: Cleaning up after smoking is, all in all, almost as time-consuming as cleaning up after eating. It isn't just those overflowing (and spilled) ashtrays and half-used matchbooks everywhere, it's the dropped butts and ashes flicked onto floors, into sinks, and even houseplants. It's holes burned in tablecloths, burn marks on coasters and plastic fixtures, and a nasty smell that permeates clothes, furniture, car interiors, and even pets; not to mention the tar deposits and yellow stain on every wall, window, and ceiling surface. If you won't quit, you can at least help with the cleanup.

9. PET POLICY: Animals can be fun to have around, but when it comes to the incidentals such as feeding, watering, kennel cleaning, vet trips, walking, bathing, brushing, cleaning up shed hair, and repairing chewed furniture, "man's best friend" is usually tended by woman (see p. 50).

10.BATHROOM BEASTLINESS: The returns are in, and they overwhelmingly indict the bathroom as a trouble spot. We men may not spend as much time in there as our better halves, but in the time we do spend we manage to leave all manner of mess and unsightly evidence of our presence. A little forethought here will go a long way (see p. 62).

Food Fallout

We all have our own candidates for Number 1 mess, but food mess is undoubtedly a biggie. Dishes three times a day is enough to drive any person over the edge, but when you add in-between meals and late-night snacks, it's like dumping a bucket of dirty mop water on your wife's head. I can remember the days when at about three in the afternoon we kids would rip into the bread and peanut butter and jam for a bite to tide us over . . . and always leave the jars open, crumbs all over, and the sticky utensils on the counter. We tided ourselves over—but we didn't tidy up the kitchen.

Most men leave snacks or short meals and food residue where they finish . . . which is no better than a feedlot pig does. The two-minute job of cleanup is now a ten-minute job for the woman. There is no excuse for this—none. It was our snack, our mess, our stomach.

Some Food Foibles to be Avoided:

Is This How Pasteur Got Started? Taking cups of coffee, bowls of chili, pastrami sandwiches—whatever happens to be on today's menu—into the shop, basement, or spare room, and leaving behind what will become an encrusted plate, moldy cup, or scummy bowl.

Ring-a-Leavio Putting wet glasses on wood furniture without coasters, which leaves an ugly (and hard if not impossible to remove) white ring.

Shell-shock Leaving shrapnel and hulls behind wherever we happen to be snacking on peanuts, popcorn, or potato chips. (I think we all know better than to eat crackers in bed!)

Wrap It Up Putting cheese, meat, etc., back into the fridge unwrapped; putting jars, bottles, etc., back without their tops or caps on. (This doesn't mean close it and put it back if *there is only a tiny bit left!*)

Sour Stuff Drinking directly from the milk or juice carton, leaving the milk or butter out on the counter.

Out of Ice Again Don't leave the empty ice-cube tray sitting out—rinse and refill it and put it back in the freezer.

Shove It When you push, shove, or jam leftovers into an already-full refrigerator, something's bound to spill. Check for wasted space or spoiled food that can be tossed out to make room.

Bacon Snitching and Beyond If you mooch all the mozzarella at midnight, how's she going to make the lasagna? *Ask before you eat it*—if it's clearly not a normal inhabitant of the refrigerator. Freezer raiding is even more insidious, because the theft isn't discovered until it's too late. You hardcore cases know who you are!

Strange Brews and Unpleasant Surprises Don't stash stuff you're hiding from the dog in the refrigerator. If you're undecided about something, throw it out *now*. And if you do put something awful in there (your ripened livers and doughbait for catfishing, a five-pound sack of grass seed) admit your guilt before it ferments or sprouts and dispose of it.

Squatter's Rights: Dresser Tops

Did you know burglars can rob a man's bedroom much faster and more efficiently than a woman's? To find a woman's treasures they have to get into drawers, search, and dig. Bagging a man's valuables and mementos is a piece of cake. All they have to do is scoop it off the top of the dresser!

Dresser tops were never officially granted to either sex, but we men somehow assumed all this territory for our tools, receipts, pens, pencils, pocketknives, cufflinks, silver dollars, golf tees, half-toothpicks, used hankies. When we reload the good stuff into our pockets in the morning, we leave the questionable things, hoping that a junk gremlin (or a woman!) will dispose of it. Let's start undressing the dresser top!

Some Closet Courtesies

We men blame all closet mess on women, but we are fully as rash and reckless with these storage spaces out of public sight. We, too, have a good part of our college wardrobe still secreted in there, along with our WWII infantry uniform and the Hawaiian shirts, Australian bush hat, and embroidered lederhosen we'll never wear. A two-foot thick Alaskan parka eats up an unholy hunk of "our space," and it stays there all year, not just during the three-month season in which we wear it at least twice. We'd have room for it, though, if we chucked our complete historical collection of tie widths, collar styles, and stained shirts.

To find the floor, we'd have to move a superstructure of bent and collapsed hangers, an assortment of jaded jogging shoes, and those good-as-new eighteen-inch cowboy boots that keep flopping over. The snorkeling equipment we never use is what we'd find at the bottom.

The only thing *not* in the closet are our clean clothes (which are still down in the laundry room waiting for a woman to reroute them, or draped on a doorknob, open drawer, or banister somewhere).

A friend of mine in North Carolina said when she discovered that her new husband left his trousers on the floor where he took them off, she kicked them under the bed. Two days later he left his work pants in the same place and she kicked *them* under the bed. After she repeated this ritual with seven pairs of trousers, the new husband's wardrobe was depleted. He came into the kitchen wrapped in a towel, saying, "Honey, do you know where all my pants are?"

"Yup. Right under the bed where you left them." For the next forty years of marriage and to this day, he's never left his trousers to be picked up.

In case you wondered,

Throw	*really means*	*Hang*
Cram	*really means*	*Fold*
Pile	*really means*	*Place*
Keepable	*really means*	*Usable*
Stash	*really means*	*Trash*

Caution: Men at Work

There is no more impressive male territorial intimidator than the workshop. It's far more forbidden territory than a woman's sewing room is to a man. All of those tools and power gizmos, the "keep away" smells of unfamiliar solvents, all those gauges, testers, and sharpeners are, by their very nature, a keep-out sign to the female. They make her feel unworthy to consider any encroachment on or to question any expansion of the area.

In reality, a lot of the apparatus in a workshop is about as hard to operate as the electric can opener in the kitchen. Isn't it amazing that for all the room it takes up, all the elaborate equipment and accessories, investment and insurance, how little ever comes out of it? I'd bet more actual fixing and parts and tools come out of the kitchen "junk" drawer than many an entire workshop.

What actually inhabits the workshop, for the most part?

dried-up caulk cartridges

important fluids in rusty cans with no labels

oily rags

dead batteries

stray blobs of solder

holey hose

dried-up cans of leftover paint

petrified paintbrushes

coffee cans half full of unidentifiable objects

unsorted nails, screws, and washers in everything but the size you need

broken parts

obsolete plumbing and unreliable electrical parts

dead machines

old license plates and hubcaps

greasy back issues of Popular Mechanics

These things aren't just fire hazards, they're ugly and smelly. Convert the junk bench back to a workbench!

Junk Knows No Gender

We men are astonishing junkers and our junk takes up much more than its share of the room. We have stuff stashed away we can't remember and that we'll never use again. All sorts of things. You would weep if you knew how many of your wives have called and written me to pour their hearts out about your junk . . . Every note you ever took in medical school, three classic cars (none of which run), twenty-five years' worth of *Modern Photography,* your great-grandfather's lawn

bowling trophies, a guitar with no strings, expensive (and ugly) collector's decanters, luckless lottery tickets, dusty and dismembered radios and TVs, the high school yearbooks you haven't looked at in thirty years, the stamp collection you were very hot on in fifth grade, the wreckage of your model of the *Santa Maria,* elaborate equipment for a succession of hobbies you've lost interest in or never gotten around to, and at least a half-pound of unidentified keys.

Clean everything out and don't worry if your wife happens to be a bigger junker than you—we all think that. The best way to get her to toss out her junk is by leadership and example. "Hey look, Joan, I'm clean

and free." Jump up and click your heels—and watch her tackle her stacks.

When you've gotten through your closets, drawers, den, glove compartment, and that cave of clutter known as the garage, you can move on to:

The Attic, Basement, and Like Storage Areas

These are always buggy and snakey and filled with heavy, bulky, ancient things. About 75 percent of this "treasure" is junk—not to mention booby traps and fire hazards—so you can safely assume the aggressor role of grubbing in and grabbing all the dead-end entities in and around these places. She can't do it or she won't (mainly because most of it is *yours* so she can't decide). Right now, burrow in and mark and murder the junk.

Throw out the trash and give the good stuff to the charity of your choice. If you can't bear to part with something, put it in an "emotional withdrawal" box and seal it. Three weeks later, you can chuck the box (you won't remember what's in there, so it won't hurt a bit).

Pet Peeves

Pets have the distinction of joint ownership, but seldom joint cleanership. When you remove *di* and *tion* from distinction, what do you have left?

Pet care involves a lot more than footing the bill for chow and licenses. Those lovable creatures, while spreading joy, also spread hair (and often worse until they're housebroken). Who do you usually find feeding, grooming, exercising, and cleaning up after an animal? Who empties the litter box, takes the pet for its shots? Yup, the woman. It's always *our* dog on the hunt, hers when it barfs after getting into the garbage. The cat is hers when it sheds and scratches, ours when it's looking for a lap to purr in. Men have always found it more macho to horse around than to actually lead the horse to water (and then stand and wait while it delicately sips ten endless gallons). About the only thing we take the initiative in here is teaching pets bad habits—such as licking dishes or leaping onto the bed or the upholstery.

And yet, from Adam's very first instructions, animal care was a *masculine* tradition. Miraculous, isn't it (not to mention convenient) how evolution has again occurred. Don't let your wife and kids get stuck with all the dirty work.

Fetch, You Female!

"*Fetch*" . . . was all we had to yell as youngsters when we wanted something and there was a beloved mom or little sister who enthusiastically dug it out and delivered it to us. Later, we only had to shoot a duck from the bank or boat and our faithful dog jumped into the icy water to bring it to our feet. In time, we assumed that all we had to do was whistle and someone would jump. Finding "fetch" a magic word, most of us then replaced Mother and Bowser with a wife.

Knowing (if not appreciating) the value of a fetching female, we've even mastered the art of subconscious suggestion, or camouflaged "Fetch." By indirect, implied means we can still bellow for her to fetch:

"**While you're up, I wouldn't mind another cup of coffee.**"

"**I think I will have a piece of pie now.**"

"**We don't seem to have enough napkins . . .**"

"**Have you seen my shoes?**"

"**Where are my clean shirts?**"

"**Where did I put my keys?**"

"**Where did you hide the scissors?**"

"**It's time to feed Fifi.**"

"**How about a sandwich?**"

"**Aren't there any pretzels?**"

"**I guess the fire is going out . . .**"

"**We're out of toilet paper again?**"

Run Your Own Errands (For a Change)

Like most of you, I run five projects ahead of my ability to execute and always need something now or yesterday that I was too busy to get, or too lazy to think of before now. Inevitably, when I feel that pressing need, I never consider doing the errand myself but call out for someone else to run and get it. In essence saying, "I'm too busy and important to take time to twink with something like this."

I was forty-eight before I suddenly realized how many times I had unthinkingly and unappreciatively yelled "fetch" to my wife and children.

At that point, with eight teenagers and a thriving business, I had eight home and farm vehicles and forty company vehicles. When the plates were about to expire, I'd holler for help, generally at the last minute, and my wife would head for the license bureau. Soon, as if by magic, a crisp current set of plates would appear on my desk. This system worked great for twenty years, until my wife happened to be visiting a daughter and her new baby during vehicle renewal time. So I decided to take care of this little detail myself. I dug the old registration out of the glove compartment and zoomed downtown . . . where there was a ghastly line. I stood in it, being elbowed and crowded with all the other fetch wives— ten minutes, twenty minutes, forty minutes, an hour. Kids were screaming and slapping all-day suckers against my new suit. A wheezing pot-bellied man behind me smoked 400 cigarettes, people were coughing,

hacking, profaning on all sides.

When I got to the clerk, I couldn't get the plates after all because I'd forgotten to bring the title. The clerk muttered under her breath, "Should have sent your wife."

I was emotionally wounded by the experience and later asked my wife if it was that bad all the time. "An hour is *good* time," she said. For twenty years, for fleets of automobiles, I'd sent her to get my plates. How could I have been that inconsiderate? It's easy when you've been conditioned all your life that it's a woman's job to fetch. I never thanked her once!

The phrase "errand boy" is one of the most ironic errors of our vocabulary. Most, if not all, errands are run by the WOMEN of the world. Just tell me who runs 90 percent of your errands—your wife, one of the kids, your secretary. Even if you're handier and have the time, you won't do it; you'll come all the way home or to the office and then send them forth.

Errands are a sacrifice of time and life. Errands take time, errands mean traffic, lines, busy telephones, indifferent or intimidating salespeople, back orders, wild goose chases.

It is *not* a privilege for someone to spend her life and time in our behalf—yet "pick this or that up for me" is an automatic reflex for most men.

You may pay someone to run business errands and that is fine, but at home, no one works for you, you work together. Programming a *please* in there would help—but not half as much as running our *own* errands at least part of the time.

If you suddenly ran all your own errands it would cause heart failure for sure, so take it easy and start by taking care of just a few. Then when your mate is adjusted to the shock, ask her sometime if you can pick up something or run an errand for her. It'll take her a while to recover, but you'll be treated sweeter.

Surrender Some Unreasonable Attitudes and Demands . . .

"We eat at exactly 6:00!"

"Not only the food but the plates will be warm!"

"Sheets are changed every other day, whether they need to be or not."

"I don't want to hear a peep out of the kids."

Just because your mother did it, the army insisted on it, or you happen to be a prison warden doesn't mean the rules are good or necessary.

Where did we men get to be "certified housework appraisers/evaluators" anyway? Certainly not from experience! My Aunt Glenda remarked, "Since we retired, after forty-five years of cleaning, I've found out I don't know how to sweep. My husband Jim now tells me I'm doing it all wrong." Our unreasonable attitudes and demands often have gestapo grimness. We don't give ourselves a certain time to do something or finish watching a football game or fiddle with a fun project—yet "she" better have "it" done on time.

What "our Mother did" loses authority with age; her floors, food, mending, and organization were probably only about half as good as we now remember them. Yet these memories form our expectations of how things should be done in "our" present home. Expecting things to be exactly thus-and-so when we come home from work precludes the possibility that everything didn't go thus-and-so for her all day!

CHAPTER 6

House-cleaning 101

Basic Curriculum Course Finally Available

At last! The course not taught in high school, college, or even continuing education curricula, a course that's required for smart and happy living. Though it has no grades, no tests, and no attendence requirements it can make life more livable than ten semesters of other courses combined.

In all of education today, the cry is "Back to the Basics." What could be more basic than keeping the things we have to use and look at every day clean and pleasant to be around?

Forgive me if these basic housekeeping instructions insult your intelligence here and there, but "I don't know how" keeps cropping up when household chores are involved. In this chapter I've tried to include all the gory details so "I don't know how" won't stand in our way anymore.

Straightening Up

Professional cleaners and soldiers call this most basic of all cleaning operations "policing the area." It's a simple matter, when passing through an area, of slowing down enough to put a few items back in order. It takes no tools or no special skills—just an observant eye and a bend of the back and knees. The average home needs to be straightened up far more often than it needs to be cleaned, so this is a talent well worth cultivating.

Unfortunately, most of us men outgrew the urge to be policemen by the age of ten. When the fair sex straightened our tie before Sunday School, we took that as an eternal commitment to straighten up every-thing for us evermore. But the Sunday School truth is that "Anyone old enough to mess up is old enough to clean up." Indeed, brethren, in this case a helping hand sure beats a praying limb.

Tackling the Tenth-Time Offenders

We men are in an especially good position to do something about the repeat offenders, the things that have to be straightened up again and again and

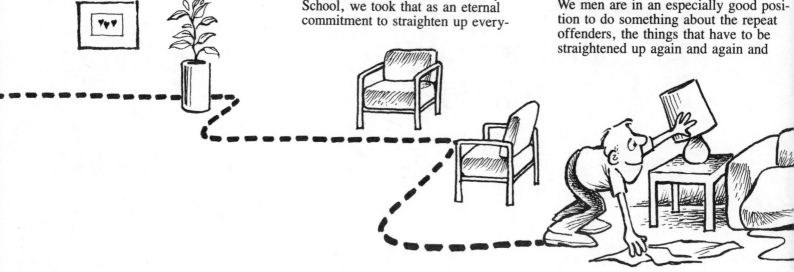

again. I'm talking about the things that are always a mess, that we seldom noticed or worried about before, because we were doing the messing up, not the straightening up. After you've rounded up scattered magazines for the twenty-ninth straight day, or raked up the droppings from the Mucho Sheddus Leafus plant, or retilted a tipped-over TV tray, you can take the initiative and say, "How are we going to deal with this?" A high percentage of litter is caused by lack of official places to park things—lack of racks, hangers, hooks, shelves, cupboards, etc. A lot of things are like little tumbleweeds or third wheels loose in the house—always lying or drifting around somewhere. We can be eternal straighteners or straighten them up in one fell swoop, forever—send them up the river or down the chute. Why don't you suspend their license to litter on your next policing patrol?

Anytime, anywhere you pass inches from a dropped newspaper, a crooked picture, an open drawer or door, a dead leaf, something spilled or wrinkled, something that needs to be tucked in, thrown out, adjusted, put back, YOU CAN AND SHOULD DO IT! It only takes seconds and when done regularly saves a big cleaning binge. Fix it up, pick it up, straighten it, *straighten up*—it'll help you go straight in life.

Make Your Bed After You Lie in It

Three years ago, awakened by a comment card from a woman in my audience, I was amazed to realize that I'd slept in a bed 18,000 times in my lifetime—and probably only made a bed about 130 times. Who made all those beds? My wife? My daughters? The maid? When I thought about it, I had to admit, in simple honest logic, that since I messed up at least half of it every day, I should probably make it at least half the time.

I could understand a man shying away from "apron work" such as dishes or laundry but a failure to pounce on the bed chores is unimaginable. Of all the places we should show respect if not *enthusiasm* for. . . . What provides the quality of experience, recreation, and security a bed does? Let's get as serious about the after-care as the foreplay.

Changing the Sheets

We'll start with this because changing the sheets is much more challenging than merely making the bed. When you change the sheets, do it like the hotel professionals—with a minimum of effort. They only walk around the bed *once*. (Unfortunately, this approach won't work with fitted sheets, which must be stretched from corner to corner of the mattress before the rest of the bed can be made.)

Stand beside the bed and spread both top and bottom sheets across the mattress. Make sure they're smooth and straight. Next comes the blanket, then turn a few inches of the top sheet back and fold it over the blanket. Now, with everything shipshape, begin your circuit of the bed.

Starting at the headboard, tuck the sheet firmly beneath the mattress. (Hospital corners are snazzy if you know how, but not necessary.) You're tucking in at least two layers—if there's a blanket, three—down one side and then around the bottom. Keep tucking—tight! smooth!—straightaway up the other side and you're home free. Now whip on that bedspread, making sure the overhang is equal on all sides and that there's enough at the head of the bed to cover the pillow plus a little slack. Why the slack? *So you can tuck it under the pillow edge*—see illustration on the opposite page—you'll never need to be intimidated by this aspect again.

Making the Bed

The day-to-day act of bedmaking is relatively simple. First, make sure that the top and bottom sheet are still firmly tucked beneath the mattress—this is where fitted sheets are time-savers. Pull up the blanket, make sure it's straight and smooth, and fold the top few inches of the top sheet over the blanket. Then repeat the tucking routine and continue with bedspread and pillows as before.

No fair taking the ostrich approach—leaving the top sheet and maybe even the blanket bunched up at the bottom of the bed and covering it up with the bedspread—out of sight, out of mind . . . except that the sheet creates a nasty lump that's only magnified by the spread.

And don't let your sheets hang out—tuck those babies in when they come loose. They look tacky peeking out from under the spread!

For those of you convinced it doesn't make any sense to make a bed "when you're just going to sleep in it again," there is a respectable way out. Minimize the number of blankets and covers you use—a couple of thick ones are better than four thin ones that you'll be half the morning smoothing and straightening out. Or buy a comforter quilt that can serve as a bedspread too.

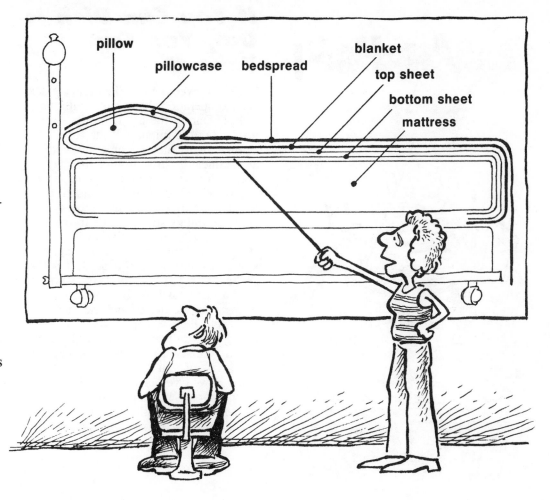

pillow · pillowcase · bedspread · blanket · top sheet · bottom sheet · mattress

AAAAHHHGH!

If You Can Dish It Out, You Can Take It

Have you ever noticed the amazing sex change operation that occurs with the dishes? During the meal, they are the man's, but the minute all the food is slurped away, they become the woman's. Since the invention of the clay pot, men have schemed ways to escape doing the dishes. They've sanded the wooden salad bowls, they've tried breaking things so they'd be thrown out of the kitchen, they've even stooped to claiming their hands are allergic to water (though it doesn't bother them to reach into the lake to unsnag a lure!). All my life the girls or women did the dishes and the men . . . well, they disappeared.

I shouldn't have to use page space to tell you how to do dishes, except that a few of you actually might not know how. I've been to your houses when your wife was gone—you washed one dish at a time or were reduced to using the souvenir plates off the wall!

Don't Be a Dish Dunce—Go for It!

1. Carry dishes to the sink.
Just taking your own (scraped) dish to the sink or kitchen counter is a help. When ten people leave it to one dish doer, it adds a lot of walking to the job of washing.

2. Never let dishes sit.
Scrape off the food: trying to wash dishes plastered with potatoes and

gravy, petrified pasta, and hardened ham rinds is like taking a bath with your clothes on.

3. Soak pans. Pots and pans and

other heavy-duty units need to soak during the meal so the burned-on crud in the bottom will soften for easier removal. And never *scour* that cast iron cookware unless you want to see how it looks with a coat of rust.

4. Dishwashers aren't robots or garbage disposals. Hard egg embedded in the silverware will be there after the process—only more solidly. Scrape and rinse dishes before putting them in the dishwasher. Unless you're dealing with lots of dishes, these automated units are slow and wasteful; you can get it done faster by hand. Likewise, garbage disposals aren't garbage disposals *unless you turn them on.* If you cram food down and don't flip the switch, all that awful stuff may end up in the dishwasher on its final rinse.

5. The hand washing process: Pile the silverware into the water when you start and let it soak till the very end, to loosen encrusted food before washing. Glass, plastic, and fragile objects should be washed first while the wash water still has its full power—and before the heavy stuff is piled into a murky sinkful. Change the water whenever it goes grubby—which might mean three times, if the main course was spaghetti.

6. Use HOT water to wash and rinse with: the hotter the better, as hot as you can stand. The old issue of who washes and who dries is in fact obsolete—after you rinse dishes under hot water, you don't have to dry them (unless we're talking about crystal goblets or other clear glass where a few water spots would be out of the question). Air drying is surely more sanitary than rubbing dishes with a damp, dirty dishtowel that's been hanging around the kitchen all week.

7. Surprise! *Cleaning out the sink and sink strainer is part of doing dishes.*

8. As is wiping the table, and the kitchen cooking area. This has long been the secret knowledge of women, but wiping the counters, stove top, fridge front, can opener, etc., is part of the job and only takes seconds when the mess is fresh—leave them till later and you'll have to chisel them clean.

A Man Can (Clean the Bathroom)

All the cheerleaders in the Senior High leaped to their feet and gave me a surprise ovation for a single sentence I uttered in an assembly. All I asked the boys was, "Why do mothers, daughters, and wives have to clean the outsides of toilets (and the floor around it) when men's inaccuracy caused the mess and smell?"

If the average man knew how much the average woman despises toilet splashes, and shaving residue in, on, and around the sink, soggy towels on the floor, and shower scum buildup, he would clean up his act, and *fast!*

I give a professional course in the art of cleaning a bathroom in three and a half minutes on page 114 of *Is There Life After Housework?* which I highly recommend you read. Lots of cleaning can be done by not dirtying the place in the first place; in ten minutes in the bathroom getting ready, we are creating thirty minutes of work. So in the bathroom, we should concentrate on three critical stages: before, during, and after.

1. BEFORE . . . We're quick to criticize a few extra cosmetic containers of hers, while our drawers and shelves have twenty ornate flasks of aftershave (eighteen of which we never use), a rancid vial of Vitamin E, thirty-two disposable razors in various stages of disposability, the shaving brush and straight razor our mother-in-law gave us six Christmases ago, several half-empty cans of shaving cream, a mildewed loofah, wet matchbook covers, rusted tie tacks, prehistoric prescriptions, ruptured tubes of hair cream, combs with missing teeth, swollen pulp novels, and a broken blow dryer. Don't worry about her stuff—clean yours out and there'll finally be room for the spare roll under the sink.

2. DURING . . . While you use the bathroom you can:

Aim . . . at the toilet and take care of "accidents" when they happen.

Take showers with the curtains inside the tub, so the floor and rug don't get soaked.

Put that cap back on, brother! It takes exactly the same time to do it now as later—except by then it will have rolled down the drain or off down the hall!

Flossing teeth—although important—will never be an Olympic event. Lodged plaque freed by the floss sails out and sticks to the mirror. If you hold your head down when you floss or brush your teeth, the spatters will end up in the sink instead of on the mirror.

If you do get something on the mirror, give it a quick blast with a spray bottle of glass cleaner, *not* a wet washrag, which will make it look twice as bad.

3. AFTER . . . Put the toilet seat back down to save your beloved the chilling experience of cold porcelain on a bare bottom in the middle of the night.

Hair in the shower, bath, or sink is about the grossest thing go-

ing. We leave it and it sticks to the side of the tub and drain, sink top, etc. Sexy, isn't it? Nope, sickening . . . ! All we have to do is stand in the tub and drip dry while we slosh water around to flush the hair down the drain.

Don't leave the wet bar-soap sitting on the edge of the tub, or the back of the toilet or sink. Put it in the soap dish.

Rinse away that stuff in the sink—whiskers, toothpaste, shaving cream, whatever. Any residue can be wiped away with a quick swipe of a nylon scrubbing sponge.

Wipe or squeegee down the walls after you shower.

Hang up your towel and washcloth, and return your sailboat to its slip.

Close all the drawers and put all the bottles and tubes back. (Metal cans will leave little rusty rings on porcelain if left sitting on the sink.)

Throw away those little scraps of tissue you've used to stop the flow of blood from shaving cuts.

And replace the toilet paper when it runs out instead of setting the new roll on top of the tank for HER to install!

Dust Busting

Dusting is a relatively simple chore we tend to think of in "take it or leave it" terms. But it's not just dust, it's dead bugs, orange pits, crumbs, wrappers, withered plant leaves, and cobwebs that accumulate gradually on almost every household surface and can eventually erode even a castle. Dusting requires no vigorous training and any man, even running on a tight schedule, still has a few spare moments to seize a dusting tool and do this nagging little operation. Ten minutes of hustling will get the dusting done!

Dusting Basics

1. You dust *before* you vacuum.

2. Dust top to bottom.

3. A once-a-week once-over-lightly is enough for the average house.

4. Monthly, hit door frames, window blinds, valances, light fixtures.

5. Dust lofts and rafters at least twice a year, using an extension handle.

Dusting is often most neglected and needed in high places that are hard for a woman to reach. Much of this is in

What Do You Dust With?

We men would never stoop to using an oily rag for dusting, and we wouldn't be caught dead with a feather duster. (Rags and feather dusters are not only ineffective, but actually worsen the problem!) Dust control was my first lesson in large-scale commercial cleaning. We used a chemically treated paper dustcloth (the Masslinn cloth) designed to pick up and hold dust and keep it out of circulation. They cost about 20 cents each and are disposable. I've spearheaded a national campaign to get this "cloth" used at home. Pick one up at a janitorial supply store and USE IT! You'll do a faster, better job.

Another good professional dusting tool is the lambswool or "rainbow" duster. It actually attracts dust with static electricity and is especially good for high places.

Called on the Carpet

We men don't participate much in carpet care; we hoof the dirt into it, lounge or wrestle on it, and maybe replace a threadbare piece once in a

stretch or reach territory—often guarded by a glaring spider or two. Even if you can't see the dust on the top of rafters or doors, or on exposed supports or beams, it's there and getting rid of it in these places will cut down on its circulation through the house. It will also discourage critters from camping out and creating further mess.

You may be able to arrange a great trade-off here: you do all the gruesome dusting (door frames, windowsills, beams, fixtures, high hardware, and rods), while *she* does the end tables, the plants, and her paperweight and telephone-insulator collection.

while—but that's about all. It's about time we got called on the carpet.

I'm not saying you should rush out and grab the vacuum away from your wife. On the comment cards I've distributed to women in my audiences, I ask these two questions: "What is your favorite cleaning task? Your least favorite?" You may find this shocking, but *vacuuming* is overwhelmingly women's favorite. Is it the only chance they get to relax and dream . . . or is it the soothing vibration . . . or the "instant gratification" of vacuuming . . . or maybe the sense of power? Who knows? But they love it, so let them have it!

Vicarious Vacuuming Thrills

1. Keep the home supplied with good machines. One out of every seven of you reading this needs a new vacuum *now!* They cost relatively little when you consider how much use they get, and how much pleasure a freshly vacuumed floor can bring.

● *Get a good upright. You can buy a Eureka upright—get a commercial model—for under $250 (see p. 91). If you spend more than $250, you're paying too much.*

Field Guide to Vacuum Attachments

In the event you *are* called upon to wield the vacuum, here is a generic guide to attachments that will end, once and for all, that embarrassing quandary: "But which attachment do I use?" Attachments are available for canister, upright, and wet-dry vacuums, but uprights tend to become awkward and tip over when you clamp on the converter needed to connect the attachments to the machine. Although they vary slightly from manufacturer to manufacturer, each species of attachment does have distinct characteristics that will aid you in identification:

1. Crevice tool: A long, narrow tube with a flattened tip to reach into those hard-to-get-at places such as corners and the crevices at the sides of appliances.

2. Dusting brush: A small, usually circular brush for blinds, windowsills, baseboards, and shelves—anything that might get nicked if those little brushes weren't there to cushion things.

3. Floor tool: A wide (approximately 12") head with brushes for va-cuuming

hard-surface floors; there is also a version without brushes for carpeting, called a rug tool.

4. Upholstery tool: A small wedge-shaped nozzle—usually without brushes—used for cleaning upholstery, stairs, and car interiors.

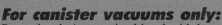

For canister vacuums only: Power head: A motorized head with beater brushes that really work that carpet over. If your vacuum has one, it will not only pick it all up—fast—but give you a sense of power and make the rug look "groomed" as well as litter-free.

For wet-drys: Squeegee head attachment for pushing water into a pool that can be vacuumed up much more easily.

● *Get a little five-gallon wet/dry vacuum. These are available everywhere now for under a hundred dollars.*

2. Maintain your machines for peak performance.

● *Change or empty bags regularly— before the vacuum begins to lose pick-up power. This is the most important thing! People tend to put it off, but it's absolutely crucial to vacuum maintenance. Replaceable paper bags are preferable for home use, but if you have a cloth bag, shake it vigorously to get all the dust out of the fabric.*

● *Replace the belt every year or so; just take a look at it from time to time and see how it's wearing.*

● *Check the fan periodically to see if it needs to be replaced. The fans in some home vacuums are scarcely recognizable as such!*

● *Replace beater bars when worn; every two or three years have the motor cleaned.*

● *Don't confuse a vacuum with a compactor. These dudes weren't designed to pick up pennies, paper clips, or vast quantities of kitty litter. When string, thread, or hair gets wrapped around the beater bar it will slow*

down the machine—turn off the vacuum immediately and remove anything that gets caught in there.

● *And don't "borrow" the house vacuum to clean up the shop or garage, or you may find yourself buying a new vacuum a lot sooner than you expected.*

3. Clean up the cow trails. The traffic patterns get dirty long before the rest of the carpet and need to be cleaned regularly to prevent unsightly paths from developing. (See *Do I Dust or Vacuum First?*, p. 62, and the revised edition of *Is There Life After Housework?*, p. 98.)

4. Shampooing is really a man-size job (chauvinistic, huh!), yet we make the wife set it up whether we're doing it ourselves or hiring it out. My expert opinion is that you pay a lot for shampooing in any case. Why not call an expert and get it cleaned right? Shampooing—if done right—actually

extends the life of your carpet. Carpet cleaning is so competitive now, the prices are in the customer's favor. You can get it cleaned quicker, better, and cheaper than you or your wife can do it. Even though I've been a professional carpet cleaner for thirty years, if I moved to a strange city and had a houseful of dirty carpet to deal with, I wouldn't rent the equipment and do it myself, I'd call a local.

5. Replace it. Carpet projects a psychological warmth; there is real emotion attached to its ownership, es-

pecially by women. The soil, wear, and damage to our carpet is absorbed into our feelings, so you really can relieve frigidity, fatigue, and rebellion by doing a surprise good deed for the carpet. Next time you get the urge to buy a fur coat, buy a furry floor covering instead! We men always ho-hum, stall, and drag our feet to avoid a carpet confrontation, forcing the women to plead for a new or better one. Nobody really wants the responsibility of deciding on a new rug, even though everyone immediately enjoys the benefits. So right now, put down this book, walk through the house, and when you see your wife say something like, "Hey, you know the carpet in the living room has been down twenty-seven years and is about uglied out, looks like we need to do something, what do you think?" (You better try this in the vicinity of the couch, because when she faints on that thin, worn-out carpet it won't absorb much impact!)

If you do these five things only, you'll be worshipped and bragged on (and you're getting off easy, you old dog, you!).

Friendlier With the Floor

A lot of years have gone by since most of you men reading this have been friendly to the floor: for most of us the floor is a vague uncharted region

where crumbs fall and parts and coins roll away. Some of us must think we have the "self-cleaning" variety, the way we let ashes, crumbs, and fingernail clippings fly!

Sweeping: You might think that good old standby, the broom, is hard to beat, but a small 12- or 18-inch commercial dust mop is far faster and more efficient on hard surface floorings like linoleum, vinyl, tile, and hardwood. It gets that fine dust you can't get with a corn broom.

Mopping: That grease on top of your fridge is also on the kitchen floor; you just don't see it because it's been worked into the pattern. You have to wash a floor like anything else or it gets dirty, cloudy, and sticky. (No matter what women claim, I know you wouldn't mop a floor without sweeping it first!)

Now here are some professional secrets for men only—you'll do it twice as fast as your woman and really freak her out. Use a neutral cleaner solution (see p. 90) with a wet mop; water alone won't cut it. Lightly wet the floor with the solution. Once doesn't do much—the first exposure to liquid acts as a wetting agent but it doesn't lift much grime. The wet shine says "clean" to your subconscious and you whip to the end brightening the floor a little but leaving a lot of residue. So wet the floor lightly, then dip the mop again in the cleaning solution. By the time you start over again, the cleaner will have dissolved and suspended the grease, and it will be released from the floor surface. Mopping may cause a tiny bit of shine loss, but a day of use will polish off the few microns of detergent residue, so don't go piling on thirty new coats of wax.

How often should you mop a floor? It depends on the use it gets, but when your bare feet stick to the floor during your late-night snack, it's past due.

Stripping the Floor: This is a gutty job; any man who would make a woman do it shouldn't be able to sit in a stadium with a clear conscience. I can strip a floor faster than a team of twelve women, and so can you. Once you master the pro way to go about this you'll be sought by all the neighbors, so keep it to yourself.

Stripping

This is to take off the old wax finish before applying the new.

1. Prepare a solution of commercial wax remover, following label directions.

2. Spread the solution on the floor in an area that you can handle at one time . . . about 10′ x10′. Then let it sit to dissolve the old hard wax.

3. Now scrub with a hand floor scrubber or floor machine with a stripping pad. Go over the area twice. (A scrape with the fingernail tells if the wax is dissolved.)

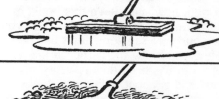

4. With an old squeegee or floor squeegee (*not* your window squeegee, see p. 90), squeegee up the dirty, mucky slop water.

5. Then scoop the sloppy puddle into a dustpan and dispose of it.

6. Now rinse. Use a little vinegar in the rinse water to neutralize the floor. This is important because the stripper is highly alkaline and if the surface isn't neutralized the new wax won't bond to it.

Wish for Wood

Whatever you do, don't let any woman cheat you out of caring for and cleaning the wood and wood paneling in your home. Caressing that luxurious grain is a downright sensual experience. The fragrance of the oil soap you use for cleaning wood beats that of a Roman bath, and the whole process soothes and restores dignity to the soul. Wood holds a mystic fear for women, so it's logical for us men to grab it. We log wood out of the mountains, we fashion it for domestic use, we might as well finish the job.

1. Don't believe the furniture polish propaganda. Ninety-five percent of women use the stuff so thick on furniture and paneling that the termites could play tag on it and never slip off. Overpolished wood gunks up and hazes out.

2. If you have raw or natural wood surfaces in your home, they'll need to be "fed," or treated to keep them from drying out and cracking. Lemon oil and other such treatments should be rubbed on. Take your time so the wood can absorb it, then wipe off the excess.

I must admit I think feeding wood is a ridiculous waste of effort and material. If grease or ink get on bare wood, it's ruined. Low-gloss or satin-sheen finishes are available that seal the surface, forming a glass-like protective membrane through which that beautiful grain will still be bright and clear and fully visible. Marks and stains will end up on it instead of on the wood.

3. If you wish to apply (or reapply) a varnish or polyurethane membrane coat to ailing wood surfaces, it's easy. First, clean the surface with a strong cleaning solution—a strong ammonia solution, wax stripper, or degreaser if it's been sealed; solvent if raw—to take off all dirt and oils. Let it dry until any swollen grain goes down. Take care of any nicks or raised spots with a few strokes of superfine sandpaper, then wipe with a tack cloth or a cloth very lightly dampened with paint thinner to pick up any dust or lint on the surface. Finally, apply the varnish or polyurethane, paying attention to the directions on the container. It may take two coats.

Here's Looking at You (Through the Window)

Have you noticed that even in your new Robert Redford running suit (with radial balance adjuster, dog mess warning sensor, and built-in blow dryer) people just don't notice you jogging down the street anymore? Jogging lost its social edge some time back and to go to all that effort without praise or pity, just for *exercise* alone is pretty grim. The everyday act of window-cleaning, believe it or not, is a hot new avenue for manly display—that is 100 percent productive as well as fun. It's been somewhat of a sleeper because it's been done with no class, with amateur tools like newspaper and vinegar. The female of the species has never really grasped the simple beauty of the job. Women dread it, they fight it, they botch it. Grab it, brethren. Window-cleaning is the most visible of all cleaning, inside or out, and it's fast and easy to do, the professional way. You are on the world's stage, you'll get all the glory! You've seen professionals turn out spotless store windows and skyscrapers in seconds. You can learn to be just as good in minutes—I promise! Those handsome brass squeegees are inexpensive and last a lifetime. Here is all you do:

Six Steps to Sparkling Windows

Go down to the janitorial supply house and buy a professional-quality brass or stainless steel squeegee with a 10-, 12-, or 14-inch blade.

Ettore Steccone brand is the best! Don't go to the local supermarket or discount house and buy those recycled truck-tire war clubs they call squeegees. These won't work well even in a professional's hands.

Pick up some window-cleaning solution, which can be either ammonia or ordinary liquid dish detergent. Either will work well if you use them sparingly.

Go to a janitorial supply house and buy a professional-quality squeegee. Make sure the rubber blade laps over both ends, and keep the blade undamaged—don't do anything but clean windows with it.

1. Put a capful of dish detergent in a bucket of warm water. There is always a tendency to add too much soap or detergent—this is what causes streaks and leaves residue.

2. Wet the window lightly with the solution, using a clean sponge, brush, or wand applicator ("Golden Glove"). You don't need to flood it. You're cleaning it, not baptizing it! If the window is really dirty or has years of "miracle" gunk buildup, go over the moistened area again.

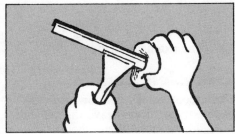

3. Wipe the dry rubber blade of your squeegee with a damp cloth or chamois. A dry blade on any dry glass surface will "peep-a-peep" along and skip places.

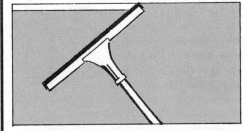

4. Next, tilt the squeegee at an angle to the glass so that only about an inch of the rubber blade presses lightly against the top of the window glass (not the window frame or the house shingles!). Then pull the squeegee across the window horizontally.

This will leave about a 1-inch dry strip across the top of the window. Remember all those drips that came running down from the top of your clean window when you tried squeegeeing once before? Well, by squeegeeing across the top first, you've removed that potential stream.

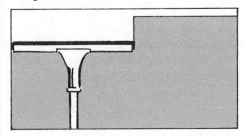

5. Place the squeegee blade horizontally in the dry area . . .

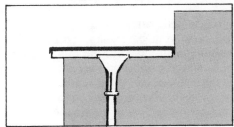

6. . . . and pull down, lapping over into the dry, clean area each time to prevent any water from running into the cleaned area. Wipe the blade with a damp cloth or chamois after each stroke. Finish with a horizontal stroke across the bottom to remove the water puddled there.

A window can be cleaned from either side or from the top using this technique. Always be sure to squeegee off that top inch of the glass first, to eliminate potential dripping. Wipe off the window sill with your damp cloth when you're finished. Exterior and interior windows are done the same.

Squeegees will work on any normal household window (not on textured or stained glass, for instance), and they can be cut to custom-fit your windows if you so desire.

What About Drips, Marks, or Lines?

"Rags" will smear or smudge.

Use your bare hand! The cleaning solution will have cut the oils in your skin and you can wipe off the small spots without leaving a mark.

As for the tiny 1/32" edge moisture, *leave it!* It will evaporate and be unnoticed.

Avoid the temptation to wipe it with finger or cloth or you'll end up with a half-inch streak.

Getting High Windows

When windows are out of reach for easy hand or ladder work, a pole or

handle of any length you can maneuver will work on the same principle with surprising accuracy. I use a 4- to 8-foot Steccone extension handle.

Extension Handle

Does second-story windows quickly and your feet never leave the ground. No ladder is needed and there's no safety risk. (See p. 90.)

Tap pole after each squeegee stroke.

Up Against the Walls

Cleaning walls and ceilings looms tall on lists of housework, but it really isn't that much of a chore. If you make regular "spot cleaning" part of your weekly household routine, they only need to be cleaned top to bottom once or twice a year. Armed with a spray bottle of cleaning solution, you can keep even with the marks on every wall, doorframe, and light switch in your house in fifteen minutes on a Saturday morning.

When the time comes to *really* get the grime off all the walls and ceilings, remember that it's a lot harder for a woman to reach above her head because of the way her muscles are arranged. So go at this job as a team: you take the ceiling and the upper half of the walls, and let her handle the walls on down. Ceilings are a snap if you get a pack of the chemical-impregnated pads called "dry sponges." With teamwork and the proper equipment, you can clean all the walls and ceilings in a big home in less than a day and actually enjoy doing it.

Washday Wizardry

Gold, solid gold. They found it lying on the ground in the wild Alaska frontier; my daughter Karla, who lives in the wilds of Skagway, Alaska, found a nice gold nugget, too, when she cleaned out the washer filter at the laundromat. Owning a classy laundromat in a town where 250 cruise ships dock yearly, she's made many amazing discoveries.

"Dad," said she who's washed the "Love Boat" captain's coat, "did you know that nine out of ten men who come in here don't have a clue how to wash clothes!"

"No!" I said incredulously.

"Do *you?*" (She dared to ask this of the world's Number 1 cleaning expert.)

My mind whipped back to the last time I tried to do laundry: when my wife Barbara was in the hospital having our daughter Cindy (now twenty-one years old). "No, I don't," I admitted. "That washer's set of dials looks like the instrument panel of a 747."

I went home humbly and tried to do a batch of wash: all nine of my best white shirts turned beige and I fried four Dacron shirts in the dryer. I know you're as tired of this ridiculous intimidation as I am, so I've consulted with expert females and reduced it all to the embarrassingly simple basics.

The Ten Commandments of Laundry

1. **Sort clothes** as follows: darks, delicate fabrics, whites, bright colors that don't run—bright colors that do or might run should be quarantined—and fuzzies (bathroom rugs and such, things capable of depositing fuzz on everything in the washload). Make sure shirt sleeves aren't rolled up, socks aren't in a ball. Turn clothes right side out—*except jeans,* which will fade less if they're inside out. *And don't wash things that shouldn't be machine washed.* Silk and wool, for example, are usually hand washed or drycleaned. Check garment tags for instructions.

2. **Pretreat stains.** Alas, stains (grass, grease, tar, tomato sauce) will not necessarily be banished by

the normal operations of washing and drying. Apply a pretreatment product according to directions and the odds are much greater that you will be able to wear your sharpest sweatshirt to the company outing.

3. Don't overload the machine. There should be enough room in the tub for the clothes to MOVE FREELY or they won't come clean. When packed in too tight, they don't get clean, and this also puts extra strain on the machine. (Even if it *does* save a few quarters at the laundromat!)

4. Use the correct cycle setting. Many washing machines have instructions for use printed on the inside lid. This will explain all the mysterious distinctions between gentle, permanent press, rinse, and spin, as well as critical basic information like how to turn the blasted thing on!

5. Use the correct water temperature. A reliable rule of thumb is hot water for whites, warm water for medium and dark colors, cold water for bright colors. If your detergent doesn't work in cold water (check the box), wash brights in warm water.

6. Don't use too much detergent. Check the box or bottle and *measure;* more is not better in this case. If you use too much detergent it won't rinse out, and the clothes will have a soap residue which can irritate skin. And do put the detergent in the dispenser or directly into the washtub *after* it's filled up with water.

7. Remove clothes PROMPTLY when cycle is finished. If you leave wet clothes in the washer too long, the wrinkles will set in and be twice as hard to iron out. Your mother was right, line drying is best for most fabrics, and the fresh scent of wind-whipped sheets and clothes is better than any fabric softener! But most people use dryers these days and only hang up the delicate clothes that shouldn't be machine dried. Check garment labels when in doubt about this.

8. Use the correct drying temperature. Some clothes should *never* be machine dried— your wool sweater will fit a four-year-old just fine if you make the mistake of putting it in the dryer.

Some garments should always dry *flat* on a towel or other absorbent surface. (If you hang them up to dry they'll stretch as well as develop unexpected epaulets on the shoulders.) Dryers are generally simpler to operate than washers; the instructions are often in plain sight on the top panel.

Do be sure to clean the lint filter before using the dryer. Not only is that wad of lint clinging to the filter a fire hazard, it prevents the machine from operating at full capacity—the clothes may not get quite dry.

9. Remove clothes from dryer promptly. Permanent press garments need to be removed while still slightly damp, or at the very least, hung up as soon as the dryer goes off. Otherwise, it's the *wrinkles* that'll be permanent! Even jeans and cotton shirts will be easier to iron if they're taken out when they're not quite dry.

10. Fold clothes and put them away. This too is part of the job. Bring along a few hangers to the laundry room—if you hang clothes while they're still hot from the dryer they'll be easier to iron.

More Washday Wisdom

● If it's not dirty, don't wash it. The average family uses 2,000 towels in a year—that's a lot of hours in the laundry room. Used towels aren't dirty, they're *wet!* A towel can go as long as a week. We can wear some work clothes several times, yet many people wash their work/yard clothes every day. On the other hand, if it's *really* dirty—muddy, greasy, or gritty—wash it separately so the rest of the laundry won't have to float in that grimy brine.

● Bleach should be added at the beginning of the wash cycle when the tub is full of water, never full strength onto dry clothes, unless you want the splotched look beloved by teenagers.

● If you can't bring yourself to actually immerse yourself in the washing process, you can at least clean out your pockets before throwing your clothes in the hamper or laundry basket. (On the floor, over the backs of chairs, draped on doorknobs or stair railings, under the bed, under the covers *in* the bed, in the closet, or in your bottom drawer definitely doesn't count. *By, on,* or *in the general vicinity of* the hamper won't score you any points, either.) Cleaning out the pockets will take on much more allure after the first time you wash your driver's license, or your season pass to the pool.

Are You a Hot-Shirt Husband?

Does your wife usually iron your shirt as you stand by the ironing board tapping your toes? I won't mention that you have fifteen shirts already pressed and hanging in the closet, but just have to have your *favorite* one. A BBC radio columnist warmed up this subject by asking the studio audience, "How many of you men ironed the shirt you're wearing now? Ten hands went up. "You're all single, aren't you?" They all were!

What is it, she asks, that happens to a man the minute he gets married that renders him incapable of ever ironing a shirt again? Do his ironing skills evaporate? No, they don't, but an iron will develops to never take care of his own cleaning.

A man's view of ironing is greatly altered by whether he is doing it or *she* is. If he's doing a shirt, front-and-collar alone is good enough any day; if she is, the whole thing needs to be done—and well. In this day of fuss-free fabrics and cheap and convenient professional service, ironing shirts is slave camp labor. Buy clothes that don't need it, and if you're insane enough to insist on 100 percent cotton, send them *out* to be ironed.

Strike While the Iron Is Hot!

1. Turn the iron on to the proper heat setting. Do read that little label on the garment, or you'll read it later and weep. You'll be glad to know that the iron itself—the print on the temperature selection—will help you out here.

● Don't be unduly impressed by the labels "drip-dry" and "permanent press." You will probably, in the famous housecleaner's term, have to "touch these up a bit" with the iron at a low setting, unless you're into the rumpled look.

● Don't use too hot an iron on synthetics or "delicate fabrics" unless you're looking for an excuse to never wear it again.

2. Place the article to be ironed on the ironing board (or pillowcase or towel if there's no ironing board in sight). Corduroy and wool are ironed inside out—unless you want crushed corduroy and shiny suits.

3. The mystic act of dampening might be desirable if the item is severely wrinkled or made of cotton or linen. Dampening simply means sprin-

kling with water—which can be done with a few fast flicks of a wet hand, if necessary.

● Steam, if you can face this subtlety of the process, is almost as good as sprinkling—and actually better on some things for banishing wrinkles. You do have to put water—preferably distilled—into the iron, to get steam.

4. A standard man's shirt should be ironed in the following order:

● Collar—back of collar first, then front

● Shoulder area or "yoke"

● Cuffs—inside first, then outside, then sleeves

● Front pieces—it's best to iron the button strip or "placket" on the reverse side first.

● Back or body, including that wretched "pleat" which you can iron or not depending on whether 1) it will show; 2) you are scrupulous.

● If you're of the stiff-collar school, send a blast of spray starch before you as you iron each piece.

5. Place the shirt on a hanger, fasten a top button, and hang it in the closet.

And We Shall Be Rewarded a Hundred-FOLD...

nearly as difficult as you might imagine. If you fold towels lengthwise first, you won't have to re-fold them before hanging them on the towel bar.

T-shirts, Shorts, Pajamas—*any clothes put back on a shelf or into a drawer.*

The Sunday Paper, if you're the first one to read it.

Socks deserve a special mention. Not a few of us have stooped to buying new socks rather than face the pairing of the old ones. Though

It's men who really have the reputation for snappy folding—those faultlessly folded regimental flags, intricate paper airplanes, and the perfect creases in our dress whites. And who, as well as a man, can correctly refold a road map? We once had the ability to perfectly fold tents, sails, and tarps, but somehow we've evolved to stuffing, draping, and tossing things. A billfold is about the only thing most of us males fold anymore. Some of us might fold the clothes in our suitcase if a woman isn't there to do it for us, and of course we can fold our arms when housework hovers. . . .

Folding is a good way to ease into housework because it can be done while doing something else, such as watching TV or swapping stories. Here are a few assignments to get us back in practice.

Towels and Washcloths.

It's time to squelch that ugly rumor that we can't fold anything we take out of the dryer. Even fitted sheets and king-size bedspreads are not

77

not exactly folding, the pairing of socks is similar and not an operation beyond technological comprehension. Women, for example, have managed to reduce this to a few simple clues of color, length, base material, and pattern.

Who's Got the Button?

I resent the accusation that we men never sew on buttons. It has nothing to do with willingness or skill—the problem is *availability*. (Notice, we always keep the loose button.) Women keep that fantastic collection of buttons, needles, and thread actually hidden from us. Give us access to those sewing items and we men will show you some precision buttonhood! Of course, a few of us may need a little refresher in the basic operations involved here.

Once you've laid your hands on that sewing basket, assemble your materials, button(s), item to be buttoned, needle, thread, and scissors.

Material Specs:

Needle Bigger is better, but a darning needle is usually too big. I use as large a needle as will fit through the buttonhole.

Thread If you're sewing a button that only has an eye on the back, you don't have to worry about the color because the thread won't show. Otherwise, match your thread to that of the surviving buttons.

If you can't find the exact color, go with a slightly lighter shade. If you're sewing on a coat or jacket button, use heavy-duty thread.

Operations:

Thread the Needle Moisten the end of the thread before attempting to insert it through the needle's eye. (Now you see why I like big needles.)

Pull the thread through the eye till the ends are even and knot the ends together so you have a double strand.

Sew the Button Back On
Place the button in the proper position to be sewn.

Start on the underside of the garment and poke the needle up through a button eye; pull the thread up through. Then poke the needle down through another eye and pull through and so on. If it's a four-eye button, check out how the other buttons are stitched (crisscrossed, side to side?) and do yours the same way.

Stitch the button at least five times; generally, the more stitches the less likely that you'll have to repeat the button-sewing procedure again soon.

If it's a button that gets a lot of tugging, leave a little slack between the button and fabric surface each time you pull through. This will raise the button up a little and make it easier to use, especially on thick, bulky garments. Even a lot of women don't know that trick!

After you've made your five

stitch-throughs, wrap your thread around the "stalk" or shank several times. Leaving the slack you need for a shank can be accomplished more easily by slipping a matchstick over the top of the button before you start. Then when you're through stitching, pull the matchstick out and you're ready to start wrapping the thread around the shank. Secure your handiwork on the backside by making a few last stitches and knotting the thread back on itself. *Mission accomplished!*

Finish the Job Clip the thread as close to the knot as possible and return those sewing supplies to the basket, NOW, before you forget, or you may not get the applause you deserve for finally getting a grip on your own lost buttons.

Begin the "Behind"

In thirty years as a husband and homeowner, despite the fact that I was a professional cleaner, I never *once* moved anything to get behind it. Why

GEE, HONEY, IT'S REALLY DIRTY BEHIND HERE!

was that? Because a little voice inside me always whispered, "That's the regular cleaner's job." All the rest of you men have heard and obeyed the same little voice. Even when we don't mind cleaning and gladly jump in, we never move or get behind or under anything, or in back of it, because we feel we are just helping out with the duties of the regular cleaner (the woman).

This of course is not our fault; it's a woman's—our mother's—who after cleaning our messy little behind, wrestled us down and cleaned behind our ears, and she cleaned under our bed, too. We grew up accustomed to not being responsible for what we couldn't see (though in our youth we might have gotten behind the cushions a couple of times to retrieve any change that might have rolled out of Dad's pockets!). In the thousands of housecleaning questions I've been asked by men and women over the years, I've never, ever had a man ask about anything that has to do with behind or under doors or appliances or furniture. I've figured out why, too. We men are natural exhibitionists. There is no credit or glory behind closed doors; men don't fight in private behind the barn or the bar, they do it in the street and often wait for the TV camera and press to get there before starting. The only behind that gets unsolicited attention from us is the female variety.

Well, brethren, we need to make up for being surface polishers and center-line cleaners, and jump into the realm of "down under" cleaning. The fact is, women really hate to get behind and under. They've done it all their lives, but it's hard on them. Getting in back of and under things always means ugly bugs and mice and spiders scurrying out. There are dead and rotten things behind and under and

in back of, and the simple strain and weight of moving appliances and furniture to get at unseen areas is, if we can excuse an outdated phrase, a job for a man. Trying to move something too heavy always results in injuries to the floors, walls, and the unit, as well as often to the person doing the trying.

This is a task that only has to be done a couple of times a year; it should be a cinch for us. So some Saturday morning, stroll into her presence and announce that you're taking on the duties of the hard-to-get-to, seldom-seen, and often-forgotten places—and then go to it. Here is a map of behinds that will yield a treasure of appreciation (not to mention two or three of the things you've been looking for all year).

Remember: If you get behind any major appliance be sure to unplug it or to be careful of the gas line. You'll live to enjoy the results.—she still likes you better than the insurance money.

STOVE: Pull the stove away from the wall; pad the feet of appliances with a towel for easier pull-out. The floor back there may be mighty grungy, so be prepared to let your cleaning solution soak for a while. Once the floor is clean,

use a vacuum cleaner to pick up any dust in the corners, and slide the unit back.

REFRIGERATOR: Refrigerator experts tell me the dust and grease that collect in the coils and fan area of a refrigerator cause the majority of the repair problems as well as reduce the life of the unit. Unplug the refrigerator, pull it out, and vacuum the "fur" (dust) off the coils. You can also use a radiator brush or a handle with a damp cloth wrapped around it. Wipe up the debris on the floor, then slide the unit back.

WASHER AND DRYER: Even a rental washer or dryer will find a way to gather a junk cache—lint, fuzz, odd objects that fell off the washer (out of the pockets you forgot to empty), things roaming or being swept across the floor, spilled soap powder, odd socks, all of this will bulk up behind. Pull out the unit, sweep up the clutter, then wash the back of the washer or dryer with disinfectant cleaner.

COUCH AND CHAIRS: These might seem simple, but they can be a real drag if you try to *drag*

them on the carpet. So lift them out (with two or three small moves, not one giant heave) vacuum and declutter behind, and replace.

BED: A certified doctor of dust said the average home accumulates forty pounds of dust annually. I'm convinced most of it ends up under the bed, where it can settle and lie undisturbed for great periods of time. Vacuums can be hard to maneuver under here, so try a slightly damp dust mop—it works great on carpet. Or move the bed over and then vacuum under.

PICTURES: Ah yes, we dust the fronts but that's about it. Once a year or so, take them down, dust the frame and back, and rehang (we men have a better eye for "level," anyway).

To do all of the behind work in the whole house will take you a couple of hours, tops. A great trade-off for five or six hours of other tedious chores. You can knock this off on Saturday morning and have a clear conscience through the whole Saturday afternoon sports marathon.

Compliance with Appliances

Most of us are impressed that ships are officially female but more impressive, if you think about it, is the sex slant of appliances. Men benefit 50 percent (or more) from appliances, yet they are all "hers": *her* washer, her stove, her mixer, her vacuum. (Did you ever hear a man call out, "Where's our vacuum, honey?") It's all "hers," right down to "her" can opener. Even the sink is "her" sink.

Ownership is probably psychologically absorbed from custodianship. Since we don't often clean them, we can ignore them until they break down. But between their first step and their last stumble there is an event called "UPKEEP," which is a manly calling. Upkeep involves cleaning up such things as dried milk down the inaccessible back or side of an appliance, dust accumulation in grills and motors, and burned, aged-on grease in the burner area. Some evening or early Saturday morning, it would be downright macho to start a relationship, a kind of vicarious infidelity, with these "she" appliances—service and clean them.

Spend More Time Soaking and Less Time Scrubbing!

To clean the exterior of any major appliance—stove, refrigerator, washing machine, or dryer—follow these easy steps.

1. Using a spray bottle, squirt on a solution of heavy-duty cleaner or grease cutter. A high butyl content cleaner (like wax remover) really works on the grease . . . FAST!!!

2. If you need to scrub, use a soft nylon pad, *don't* use scouring powder, steel wool, rugged nylon pads, or metal scrapers. You'll scratch the finish.

3. Let the cleaning solution remain on the surface for a while to soften and dissolve the dirt and grease.

4. Then wipe it off with a soft towel or cloth. If you want the unit to really shine, spray it with glass cleaner, and wipe again.

Stoves

Stoves require some special treatment in addition to the above, because grease droplets and burned-on stains are really tough to remove.

1. Start by taking the burner pans out, if possible, and soaking them in hot, soapy water while you're cleaning the stove top.

2. Your nylon pad or sponge will take care of the softer baked-on grease, but you may need to resort to a curly metal strand pad ("Chore Boy") to get rid of those encrusted grease droplets. (The sharp edges of the pad will pick up the bumps, and if you keep it wet it won't hurt the surface.) Rinse the pad occasionally with hot water to remove the accumulated grease.

3. Then rinse the burner pans and replace them. (They may need a little scrubbing yet.)

4. Wipe the stovetop, front, and sides with glass cleaner, and your stove will sparkle like new.

Conquering the Caves

Houses are full of hidden places that provide an invisible serving of housework. We men constantly pass by the outside, almost never experiencing beyond. *Someone has to go in there—* why not us for a change? What gentleman would send his lady down in the mine, through a dangerous tunnel, into a chasm of beetles and bats! Here are some house caves to explore and de-chore!

The Unspeakable Oven

First of all, don't believe *anything* comes "off easy." No matter what you use, including "miracle overnight soako's," this is going to be hard, dirty work. As professional cleaners using the same types of chemical oven cleaners you do, the only magic we've found is patience. Dope those sticky dudes down and don't be overanxious to get to the wiping off. Make sure there's plenty of ventilation; let the solution work even longer than it says on the label. It will almost surely save scrap-

ing and grinding. I like nylon scrubbing pads (such as Scotch-brite); they whip into the pesky spots around the elements, corners, and cracks. *Here's the secret women never knew*—when it

all doesn't come off, it means the solution ran out of oomph before it dissolved all the grease. So instead of violently scrubbing the remaining spots, just apply a second coat of solution and you can wipe it off in seconds (after you *wait*)!

Fridge and Freezer

A man is about as likely to enter these enclosures to "clean 'em out" as he is to intentionally walk into a women's restroom. Refrigerators are the acknowledged domain of the female (though we may actually use the fridge more).

Should you be able and willing to face "the big cleanout"—it does take a strong stomach and nerves of steel—here is the procedure.

1. Take everything out of the refrigerator.

2. Mix a solution of 1½ oz. ammonia or disinfectant cleaner in 3 gallons of water.

3. Wash all surfaces with a soft nylon scrub sponge; wet down and sponge off hardened food.

4. If possible, remove the wire shelves, the vegetable bin, and the cooler try and wash these in the sink.

5. Then dry and buff all areas with a soft, clean cloth, and replace contents of refrigerator.

The Cooking Vents and Grilles

Cooking grease, dust, etc., are constantly sucked into kitchen vents. A vent can get a half inch thick with grease and become smelly, as well as a real fire hazard. I've cleaned thousands of vents professionally—it only takes a few minutes and you can and should (about once a year) take care of this ceiling cave.

First unscrew the cover plate or grille. Put it in a sink full of hot water and strong grease cutter such as ammonia or wax stripper along with any filters there may be. Let them soak while you work on the rest of the unit. Next reach up into the exhaust opening and unplug the unit—the motor and fan should slip out easily. Clean off the grease with paper towels and a spray bottle of degreaser solution, being careful not to wet anything electrical or spray anything into the motor. Now spray off the grille and filters with steaming hot water. Dry everything thoroughly and reassemble. Replace the charcoal filter in non-vented units as necessary.

For years we could get an A grade in housework by performing the sole, simple act of taking out the garbage. (Even so, we didn't necessarily do it, of course.) Our new cleaning consciousness obviously calls for some revised standards here.

84

OFFICIAL GARBAGE HAULER'S PERFORMANCE APPRAISAL FORM

Aspects of Performance to be Considered	Far Exceeds Job Requirements	Exceeds Job Requirements	Meets Job Requirements	Needs Some Improvement	Does Not Meet Minimum Requirements
TIMELINESS	Empties it before the first Kleenex hits the bottom of the bag	Empties the garbage every day, or the minute it contains smelly paint rags or a rotten fish	Empties the garbage when it's full	Empties the garbage when it overflows	Empties the garbage when it fills the front room
INITIATIVE	Looks for opportunities to take out the garbage	Empties garbage without being asked	Empties garbage when asked	Empties garbage when threatened	"Garbage? What garbage?"
THOROUGHNESS	Scrubs and disinfects garbage cans every week	Puts in a new liner every time he empties the can	Takes garbage cans to curb every week and brings the empty cans back	Takes garbage cans to curb every week	Couldn't tell you what day garbage is collected
FORM	Sorts garbage into recyclables and trash	Picks up his failed backboard and rim shots and deposits them in the can.	Drops things on the way to the dumpster, but picks them up	Drops things on the way to the dumpster and leaves them lie	Can't even find the dumpster
ATTITUDE	Buys stock in landfill corporation	"It is *MY* job to handle the garbage"	"I will *help* with the garbage"	"Only when it's my turn"	"I don't do garbage"

CHAPTER 7

It's only natural...
for Men to find a better way

The Importance of Good Tools and Equipment

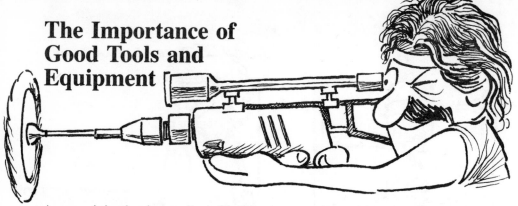

A gross injustice is usually inflicted on the housecleaner in this area. Over and over, in home after home, I see an old rattletrap vacuum, hardly capable of running, let alone sucking up any dirt. Every day we wrestle with these machines doing the housework, while in the basement or garage sits a $400 radial-arm saw or other power tool we haven't used in six months. These tools give our masculinity an occasional boost—while we fight an unsafe, ineffective vacuum for hours every week! Take a walk into your kingdom of things and you may find it a little embarrassing that you have routers, special wrenches, compressors, etc., that save a little time once or twice a year, while in the kitchen or laundry room your family struggles on, day after day, with antiquated tools and equipment.

In most cases, after an industrious project or two, we seldom use our expensive hobby gadgets and tools; as investments go, such tools are poor ones. *Our time is our most valuable commodity,* and good housecleaning tools and equipment can save hundreds of hours a year.

For a modest investment, for example, you can buy and install a built-in vacuum system for your home, making it easy and inviting for all the family to vacuum. Husbands and wives should take a serious look around their houses. The tools likely to be used most and those capable of saving the most time are the ones that should be purchased. Avoid "trinket" attachments to cleaning machines or appliances of any kind. Stick to solid basic tools and supplies.

And Ah, The Economy of it All!

There are more benefits from using the right equipment and supplies than merely doing a faster and better job.

There is SAFETY: you will be using fewer, simpler items that will be safer to use and store.

COST: you will spend 75 percent less on cleaning supplies if you select and use them properly.

DEPRECIATION: using proper cleaning supplies and tools reduces damage to and deterioration of the surfaces and structures you're cleaning.

STORAGE: few apartments, mobile homes, or, for that matter, houses have enough storage space, and the right items will be much less space-taking than the arsenal of cleaning preparations you're using now.

There are some good inexpensive tools that should be in every home to make cleaning easier. Now, don't go buying these for Mother's Day or birthdays; this isn't *her* gift, it's for the *family. . . .*

It's Only Natural . . . For Men to Buy Equipment

Especially the right kind that saves time and money on housework and does a better job. You—yes you, Mr. Ordinary Citizen—can buy professional cleaning supplies and equipment. It's easy and it's a MAN's job, because:

1. Most professional supply houses—janitorial supply stores—are in warehouse districts (tough neighborhoods).

2. You can get directions and instructions directly from the pros.

3. The technical and/or mechanical aspects of product selection here should come easy to us.

4. The supplier and dock people are more comfortable dealing with men.

5. The calendars alone are worth the trip!

Mail order, which can be done conveniently from home, is also a great way to go. I'll send you a free catalog of professional supplies and equipment if you write to me at Housework, Box 39, Pocatello, Idaho 83201.

What Can a Man Do?—Replace It!

We easily accept the fact that brakes, tires, clothes, and footwear have a natural lifespan and have to eventually be replaced, but household things we somehow envision lasting forever. *They don't!* Homemakers by the millions are battling worn-out tubs, damaged drawers, and shot screen doors. Because drapes just hang there, we figure they should last forever.

NOT SO! Even "indestructible" concrete sidewalks crack, flake, and deteriorate and not only look bad but require twice the time and expense to keep up. Toilets wear out, light fixtures often have a short lifeline. If we men did nothing but keep the household equipment and structures in fully functional condition, that alone would be an untold aid to housework.

A good example is the cookstove top. In thousands of homes I've seen stovetops with a stained and chipped surface, non-working dials, rickety knobs that are cracked or lost, and griddles blackened beyond belief. Yet because at least three of the burners will heat (with a little coaxing and some clever juggling), it stays. A new, safe, and much more attractive top only costs $150-$200!

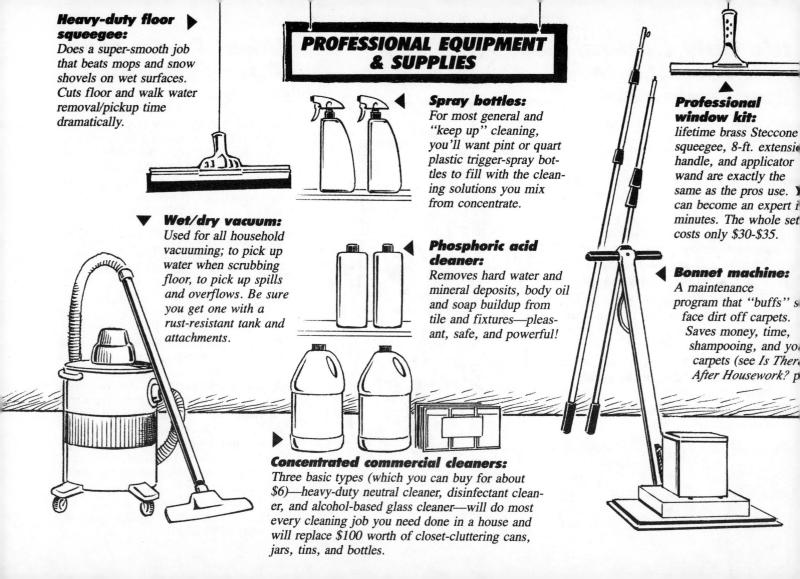

Heavy-duty floor squeegee:
Does a super-smooth job that beats mops and snow shovels on wet surfaces. Cuts floor and walk water removal/pickup time dramatically.

PROFESSIONAL EQUIPMENT & SUPPLIES

Spray bottles:
For most general and "keep up" cleaning, you'll want pint or quart plastic trigger-spray bottles to fill with the cleaning solutions you mix from concentrate.

Wet/dry vacuum:
Used for all household vacuuming; to pick up water when scrubbing floor, to pick up spills and overflows. Be sure you get one with a rust-resistant tank and attachments.

Phosphoric acid cleaner:
Removes hard water and mineral deposits, body oil and soap buildup from tile and fixtures—pleasant, safe, and powerful!

Professional window kit:
lifetime brass Steccone squeegee, 8-ft. extensi handle, and applicator wand are exactly the same as the pros use. Y can become an expert i minutes. The whole set costs only $30-$35.

Bonnet machine:
A maintenance program that "buffs" s face dirt off carpets. Saves money, time, shampooing, and yo carpets (see *Is Ther After Housework?* p

Concentrated commercial cleaners:
Three basic types (which you can buy for about $6)—heavy-duty neutral cleaner, disinfectant cleaner, and alcohol-based glass cleaner—will do most every cleaning job you need done in a house and will replace $100 worth of closet-cluttering cans, jars, tins, and bottles.

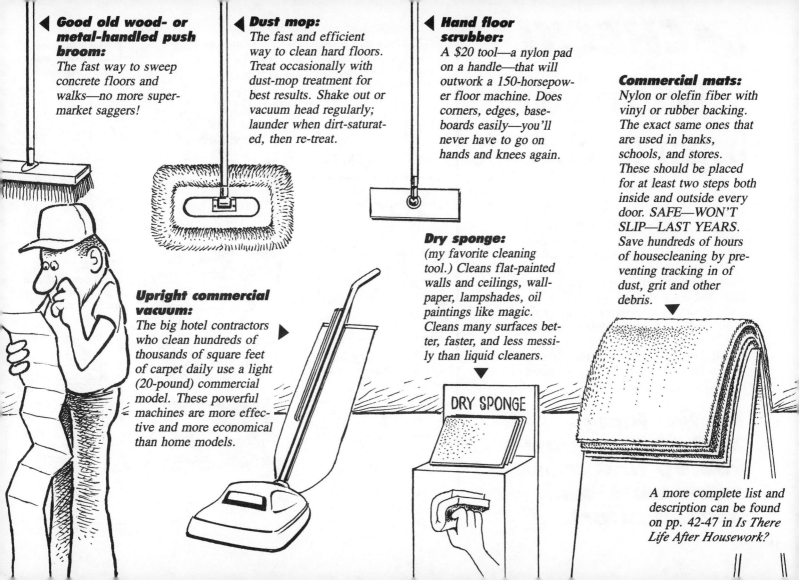

Good old wood- or metal-handled push broom:
The fast way to sweep concrete floors and walks—no more super-market saggers!

Dust mop:
The fast and efficient way to clean hard floors. Treat occasionally with dust-mop treatment for best results. Shake out or vacuum head regularly; launder when dirt-saturated, then re-treat.

Hand floor scrubber:
A $20 tool—a nylon pad on a handle—that will outwork a 150-horsepower floor machine. Does corners, edges, baseboards easily—you'll never have to go on hands and knees again.

Commercial mats:
Nylon or olefin fiber with vinyl or rubber backing. The exact same ones that are used in banks, schools, and stores. These should be placed for at least two steps both inside and outside every door. SAFE—WON'T SLIP—LAST YEARS. Save hundreds of hours of housecleaning by preventing tracking in of dust, grit and other debris.

Upright commercial vacuum:
The big hotel contractors who clean hundreds of thousands of square feet of carpet daily use a light (20-pound) commercial model. These powerful machines are more effective and more economical than home models.

Dry sponge:
(my favorite cleaning tool.) Cleans flat-painted walls and ceilings, wallpaper, lampshades, oil paintings like magic. Cleans many surfaces better, faster, and less messily than liquid cleaners.

DRY SPONGE

A more complete list and description can be found on pp. 42-47 in *Is There Life After Housework?*

CHECK!

...Before you begin to clean it.

Some things can't be cleaned. Others will look tacky even when they're clean and orderly. Taking care of these things first will make cleaning and maintenance a lot easier. It'll also get these nagging little items off your "TO DO" list once and for all.

Eliminate or remove anything that bugs you, that's inconvenient, no longer functional, or you just don't like. REMEMBER—the first principle of efficient cleaning is not having to clean in the first place.

Fix the things that always slow you up and cause extra work and wasted effort.

☐ Make sure there are plenty of wastebaskets and trash receptacles.

☐ Be sure all entranceways to the house are matted.

☐ That every leaky or dripping faucet is repaired.

☐ Label all fuse boxes.

☐ Drawer hardware is tight; drawers slide easily.

☐ Paint all surfaces that are hard to dust, wash, or clean.

☐ All dirt and air leakage into the house is stopped.

☐ All windows slide open and shut easily (and lock) and cracks are closed.

□ *Make tops of all doors smooth and dustable. Light sanding and two coats of varnish or polyurethane will do it.*

□ *Get rid of or add some padding to all head and shin bumpers.*

□ *Stair railings, clotheslines, etc., are all tightened.*

□ *Cooking exhaust is vented.*

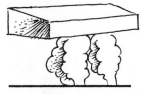

□ *All concrete floor and unfinished wood surfaces are sealed for easy maintenance.*

□ *Eliminate any furniture you aren't using or don't need.*

Old rough walls, chipped paint, cracked windows, and leaky faucets all make work. Most of us don't mind wiping a fingerprint or a black mark off the wall if a swipe of the cloth will do it, but if it's a roughly textured or cheaply painted surface, cleaning will be put off indefinitely.

Faulty household furnishings and fittings can inflict an instant pre-defeat on those who clean them. The fact that most men haven't done much cleaning is the easy explanation for why these things are still being cajoled and cuddled along. It's the woman who's always trying to squeeze another ounce, inch, or hour of life out of them (while we men are treating a buddy to a hunting trip or a football game). It amazed me how fast I found inexpensive replacements when I finally had to sweep, scrub, or clean a long-gone gadget.

Be a Man— Replace it with Something New, Better, Nicer, and Easier to Clean

Little or no expertise is needed, and often very little cash! Do-it-yourself stores are dripping with new, smarter, safer, and stronger structures! New is easier, emotionally and physically, to care for!

Improved Storage— Better than a Room Full of Roses

You can design or build things to make the house easier to clean and live in, or just to make more room! If you've been trying to come up with the ultimate gift or act to impress your companion, if dinners, fur coats, and flowers have been falling flat, lead her blindfolded into a giant new "just for her" storage area. Whip off the blindfold, and the scream of delight will be unequaled. We men make fun of the female's crammed junk storage, when the truth is we men have the majority of cubic feet. A friend was ranting that his wife filled every crack with sewing, recipes, souvenirs . . . in the next breath he said all I have is the shed out back, and the garage (790 cubic feet— his wife had four closets and under the stairs—91 cubic feet). And when the kids come back home for a visit, or leave a few things till they see how the move or the new job works out, etc., in whose space do they pile their junk?

Don't try to find more storage space in the existing structures; women can do that by instinct. *Make* more storage space.

1. **Convert no-longer-used rooms into live storage**
2. **Shelves mounted on wall standards can create a lot of new space in spots where you need it most**
3. **Build or install cupboards or shelves in those cluttered but underused areas like the basement, attic, and garage.**
4. **Move seldom-used, seasonal, or never-used stuff to the upper rafters (better yet, throw it out)**
5. **Yes, consider a little pre-fab shed in the backyard**

If worse comes to worst, sacrifice some of yours. Lack of good convenient storage space is the single biggest complaint I get from women at my seminars.

You Can Design or Build Housework Out

Use "maintenance-free" materials when you remodel or build. These are often the opposite of what we expect. A few examples:

GLASS: is great. You don't have to texture it, sand it, or paint it. Kids won't write on it, you don't have to hang pictures on it, it doesn't depreciate, and no matter how dirty it gets, it's "psychologically clean." The only thing glass needs is to be cleaned once or twice a year and we men can do that with a squeegee in a minute.

MASONRY: Beauty is in the promise of function, and from that point of view masonry may just be the most beautiful material. It insulates well, it can't be destroyed, it won't burn or rot. Its strength gives a sense of security as it resists all manner of physical abuse.

People tolerate even soiled concrete because it serves unyieldingly—flyspecks blend in with the surface and a few cobwebs give it class.

LAMINATE: We should all give our homes a little "plastic surgery." Today's laminates can look so much like wood, iron, or fabric that they fool even mother nature. Plastic surfaces resist just about all stain and soil, and we can find a shiny or textured plastic finish to match our every aesthetic want and whim. Laminate resists mars, kids' cars, sun, food, and pet attacks. It's a true maintenance-free material, and here to stay!

Bear in mind, when you're designing or remodeling, that the more different kinds of materials and surfaces you have in a room, the more equipment and *time* it will take to clean it.

CHAPTER 8

Professional Help:
Give it or get it

CLEANING AND COOKING are the big ones that can send any woman packing, especially if she's trying to cope with the other demands of a family and/or an outside job. We all know that the recent explosion of fast food restaurants has taken some pressure off the feeding end, but few of us know the cleaning industry has also provided a giant home relief valve. There are crews and companies that can clean your house faster, better, and cheaper than you could yourself. Sometimes calling in the professionals makes the same wonderful time-saving sense as junking an old wringer washer and investing in an electric model. In the busy world of jobs, career, and children, some outside help can be a savior, and it's not out of reach of the common man. You think she'll be insulted? NO WAY! What do you think she'd take if you gave her a choice between a once-a-week dinner on Saturday night at $50 or a once-a-week maid for $35 and the extra $15 in her pocket?

When to Call

In everybody's life, there's a time to call for help. I'd call when:

1. There are time limitations—the housework is becoming overwhelming because of all the other things you and your spouse *have* to do.

2. There are physical limitations—your place is just too big for the pair of you to handle, or one or both of you is somehow restricted in the kinds of physical tasks you can undertake.

3. A job is too high, too big, too special, or you just don't have the knowledge to do it.

4. Renting or finding the equipment will cost more than hiring someone to do it.

5. You just want to give a thoughtful, heartwarming gift . . . wow!

What Kind of Professional Help?

As housework is often more than whisking up a bit of dust and adjusting an off-center lamp, so is there a differ-ence in the types of professional peo-ple you can hire to come and do "your housework." Many maid services are essentially a sort of skim service. They often won't do any of the real house-work like cleaning outside windows, ovens, carpets, washing walls, or strip-ping and waxing floors. They may do these "big jobs" for a special hourly rate, but usually they just scoot in and dust, vacuum, straighten, touch up—and go.

Maid services charge by the hour (usually in the range of $20-$25 an hour) or by the visit. Should you use a franchised service or an independent? Independents have both more to gain and more to lose by pleasing you—or not pleasing you. Think about what the services offered will be worth to you, not only in terms of cost but in terms of time freed for other things. The cost to you will depend on how many hours of maid service, how many times a week or a month, your household needs to prevent minor chores from backing up. You may even decide that since you (or your kids) can do the same work just as fast for nothing, you'd rather spend the time than the money after all. By doing it yourself you'll eliminate lots of arranging and key-handling and home life interruptions. There's no home cleaning job a man can't do well . . . if he wants to!

Hire a maid service on a one-shot, trial basis to begin with. You might get a dud the first couple of tries, but give it a month or so and you'll find someone reliable who works at a reasonable rate. When you find somebody good, talk to them about returning weekly, monthly, or whatever. You need service you can count on, and if those you hire know they'll be getting regular work, they can give you a better price.

A professional cleaner (as opposed to a maid service) is the heavy-duty dude. These guys do more than briskly brandish aerosol and pine scent, they do the big heavy jobs calling for big heavy equipment. Call pro cleaners when you have a big, one-time, or seasonal job.

Who to Call

There are thousands of cleaning companies in the Yellow Pages, in newspapers, in classified ads, and on laundromat bulletin boards everywhere. Cleaning and maid services have multiplied dramatically in the last ten years. But a little caution is called for here—some

of these "professionals" are experimenting amateurs and some (more than we fellow professionals would like to admit) are destruction on wheels and casters.

Don't fall for inflated claims, including the classics: "We're big enough to do anything and small enough to care," etc. Remember, reputation is the most important criterion for selection—and for your protection. When you're shopping for a service, whether long or short term:

1. Ask them how many years they've been in business. This isn't a foolproof indicator, but it helps. In this business, there's a very high failure rate, and the people who make it and stick with it through five years are generally reliable and competent.

2. Get three to five references and call them. This *is* worth your time, because you may be selecting someone who'll be doing your work for the next twenty years, or you may be risking a $500 couch or chair—if they ruin it, it's your problem. Remember, workmanship isn't insurable: you'd have to sue.

3. Ask who will actually *do* the work—will it be the person whose

name is on the business card, the wonderful friendly voice on the phone, or will the job get farmed out to three thugs and two grade-school dropouts who'll be smoking up a storm and kicking your cat around? Know what you're getting into, to eliminate unpleasant surprises later.

Get a Bid

For big, one-time jobs, get a bid. I'd never have a cleaning crew working for me by the hour. With a bid, both parties know well in advance what they're in for. Bids are usually quoted in terms of square feet (to be cleaned, shampooed, stripped, whatever). Have a complete list of what you want done ready. Don't leave this part to them, or they'll pick the fast, easy, profitable jobs and leave the tough ones for you. Have them outline exactly what they'll do, for how much. If they're competent and professional, they'll know how long each part of the job will take and how much it'll all cost. If they can't or won't give a firm estimate, I personally would call somebody else. Getting an estimate is very simple, but SUPER IMPORTANT!

And when you get their bid (written and *signed*), be sure you check on their insurance coverage. Are they carrying *liability insurance* (in case there's an accident, they burn the house down, break out the front window, or have a fight and kill each other)? Remember, it's all going on in your house and *you* are responsible if they don't have their own insurance coverage. You are also responsible for avoidable hazards in your home—so make sure Ferocious Fido is safely out of the way for the day.

Schedule It

Here is a big one. You need to say exactly when you want the crew to come, both the day and the time. Do you want to make the neighbors nervous or irritate the street sweeper when the cleaners' van is parked in the wrong place at the wrong time? Do you want them to arrive at 2:30 when your son's graduation party starts at 3:00? Make sure about the scheduling beforehand—theirs, and yours. Tell them which door to use and make sure the arrangements for how they will get in and out are clear and firm even if you expect to be home—sudden emergencies, like a sick child or pet, *do* have the habit of popping up just when the cement patcher or the furnace cleaner is due. I once opened a door and a million-dollar cat leaped out and took off.

Three hours, eight garden trompings, and sixteen fences later the Great Cat Roundup ended successfully in the rafters of a neighbor's garage, but it wasn't exactly productive or profitable for me or my client. If you've made your arrangements beforehand—giving a reliable neighbor a key, for instance—you'll be as ready as you can ever be for the sudden disruptions of life.

Caution: If the crew doesn't have equipment and wants to use yours, I'd get a little nervous. Personal maids and friends might get by with this approach—but professionals, never. If they don't have the stuff, chances are they won't know how to use it properly either.

As for quality control, use your common sense—you know approximately how long it takes you to do these household tasks, see how the pros compare. If they take too long you know something's wrong. It's best not to stand over and watch them as they work, but you'll definitely want to inspect the job afterwards and make sure it's up to snuff.

Payment

Never, never pay in advance. We pro cleaners don't expect it or deserve it.

Pay when the work's complete, and you've checked it thoroughly. And, speaking of checking, always pay by check—it's the perfect receipt and record that the work was done, that you were satisfied, and that they actually were the ones who came and did the work.

MOST CLEANERS CAN AND WILL RESPOND TO WHAT YOU EXPECT. . . . DEMAND IT AND YOU'LL GET IT!

Becoming a Professional Cleaning Man

Sure, it's possible. If you've been working with or watching cleaning people around you at your office (and I know some of you have been muttering under your breath . . . "Scrud, I could do that and I hear they make lots of money"), take heart. Since you've started doing housework you've found out it really is fun and easy and besides, you're fast (your wife, of course, is bragging you up to keep you hustling).

Well, you're right; you can do your own thing in this business—for a few years, or for the rest of your life. If you get good at cleaning you might as well make a little profit. It's a great way to start a business the family can get involved in, and get some tax advantages as well. I cover the basics of the process in Chapter 17 of *Is There Life After Housework?*. The janitorial and cleaning industry is one of the oldest and largest professions in the world, and career opportunities abound in it. The need and opportunities for management and leadership in this industry are endless. Few, if any, jobs available today offer greater challenge, stability, and potential. Management longevity and compensations match and surpass most other industries.

If this has been enough to whet your appetite to not only clean your own home but tackle the entire township and you want more information, I have a starter kit with booklets, directions, bid tables, and information about licenses, etc. Don't buy franchises or pay to buy a cleaning business without careful consideration. One woman who bought a $15,000 maid franchise told me she'd discovered that Chapter 17 of *Is There Life After Housework?* has more and better information for $7.95 than her franchise sold her.

Write to me:

CHAPTER 9

Okay guys, take a breather, or revitalize yourself with a bit of straightening-up exercise, and let her read this next section.

FOR WOMEN'S EYES ONLY...

How Any Woman Can Feed the Flame

Now that he's read this book, he won't be able to enjoy a Monday night football or lounge lizard afternoon with a clear conscience when there's undue housework around. Once consumed with the fires of repentance we men want to, and will, do better, but gadfreys, please do leave us some pride. No matter how old we are, a little help will be appreciated—especially with things we've never done before. One fired-up woman confronted me once and said, "If I could have one wish granted, I couldn't wait to die. I'd like to come back and just sit in the kitchen and watch old George flub and grope around!" Two weeks ago, while my wife was attending a week-long seminar I performed pretty badly in the kitchen myself, and was glad she wasn't sitting there in flesh or spirit.

On the spur of the moment I decided to have an "all-fresh" dinner and made a raid on the garden and the henhouse. I'd never cooked many fresh things but I did remember she boiled the corn so I heated up a big kettle. I was going to boil beets and some eggs, too, and figured it was a waste to crank up three pots at once. So I just chucked the beets, eggs, and corn all in the boiling water. Timing never occurred to me, nor color. I ate overcooked red corn on the cob with undercooked beets and Easter eggs ready three months in advance.

I mentioned my little meal marathon to my wife when she returned, and the next day my daughter, mother-in-law, and three women from the church were all snickering and hee-hee-ho-hoing around, and dropping little remarks my way. If you get a saucepan or squeegee into our fist, you ought to do everything possible to keep it there! Here are a few suggestions to keep the embers of domestic ardor burning brightly:

1. *Tell us what you'd like done,* instead of expecting us to read your mood and mind.

2. *Be specific.* Don't just wail "I need help" without saying *what;* if we forget more than twice, you are authorized to yell.

3. *Let's sit down together and decide what the priorities are.* House cleaning can be a chance to work together toward a common goal. What you learn about compromise and cooperation here will carry over into other areas of your relationship.

4. *Give us a choice* of several jobs to get us started. Don't give us the yuckiest job first. You could kill our desire to clean in its infancy.

5. *Don't hit below the apron belt,* trying to PROVOKE us into doing, and that includes nagging. Ask graciously and we'll perform graciously.

6. *No dying-dog guilt trip* either: no eye-rolling, sighing, or menstrual-cramp faking.

7. *Remember we're only rookies.* You may need to explain how to do it.

8. *To each his own.* You have your way of doing things, so let us have our way (even if you find it funny), as long as we get the job done.

9. *Don't expect a miracle.* Just because we've been hoarding all that housework talent for twenty or forty years, we can't redeem ourselves in a single cleaning surge.

10. *Criticize privately* when we ruin, break, or streak something (*not* in front of the kids, my friends, the neighbor's wife, or your mother)!

11. *The power of positive feedback.* Remember how miffed you were when we failed to notice the job that took you all day? Don't make us go through that; we couldn't take it. Please do notice and praise us. We are going to need it!

Change

Is a magic word that can fuse joy into a humdrum life. The act of abandoning old habits and inherited prejudices (even the ones called traditions) will bring an incredible sensation of freedom. The way "they always did it" is not the way "we must always do it." Deciding and committing to finding a better way is a personal glory second only to the promise of eternal life.

In this book I've tried to take a fresh new look at some calloused old bondages and some changes I've made to clean up my own act. Those changes have enriched my own life a hundred times over, and I'm confident that applying the principles in these pages will do the same for you.

I went through a lot of years of life thinking flowers were sissy, that country music was the only good sound. I'd have to be caught dead at a drag race or wearing jogging shoes. For years, I never ate olives or avocados and I couldn't stand opera; for half my life I avoided interacting with some races and organizations because of childhood conditioning. And I figured bed making, dish doing, and errand running were beneath the dignity of a real man.

Change is a marvelous force and contribution to life and it doesn't have to mean you've jettisoned your integrity. Today I order forget-me-nots fearlessly and bend my ear to Berlioz. I wear my Nikes to demolition derbies, listen to opera on tape (in Italian, too). And I look forward to leaving the bed neatly made and to my hands getting a little rough from doing dishes. . . .

Don Aslett

About the Author

Since his birth in a small town in southern Idaho, Don Aslett has pursued every channel of opportunity available to him. When he was fifteen, his parents assigned him to operate eighty acres of the family farm; he still found time to participate enthusiastically in high-school athletics and church and community projects. Don left the farm for college knowing how to work for the other guy, but soon launched his own career in professional cleaning, organizing a group of college students into a housecleaning and building maintenance company called Varsity Contractors. Today it is a multimillion-dollar operation that spans twelve states. Don is also the owner of a maintenance consulting company whose prime client is the Bell Telephone System. In addition to his ventures in the strictly business quarter, Don presents more than 100 "Life After Housework" seminars throughout the United States each year and millions of people around the world have seen, heard, or read about him through TV, radio, and newspaper interviews.

His first book, *Is There Life After Housework?*, has sold more than half a million copies in the U.S. and England and been translated into German,

Dutch, Swedish, and Hebrew. Don followed with *Do I Dust or Vacuum First? (and 99 Other Nitty-Gritty Housecleaning Questions)* and *Clutter's Last Stand,* both of which have passed the 100,000-copy mark in sales.

Acknowledgments

I'd like to admit here that women did do some straightening up, dusting off, polishing, and fetching for this book. Especially my favorite editor, Carol Cartaino, her favorite editor, Beth Franks, and Tracy Monroe. As oldest daughters and big sisters they were entirely at home with the subject.

Men did lend a helping hand, of course. Such as Mark Browning, who cheerfully answered all those nagging little technical questions. And Craig LaGory, who not only illustrated but designed and laid out this book. He managed to make a difficult subject appealing, even fun, against his better judgment at times.

GET MORE CLEANING HELP WITH DON ASLETT'S OTHER BESTSELLING BOOKS:

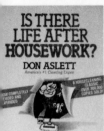

These books make great gifts for weddings, showers, or any special occasion, so use these coupons to order today!

Step-by-step instructions and diagrams show you how to clean every area of your home—and cut out up to 75% of your cleaning time! 192 pages, $7.95, paperback

It's time to de-junk your home and your life! Aslett provides all the inspiration, ideas, and encouragement you need in this fun-packed, eye-opening book. 276 pages, $8.95, paperback

You'll find answers to the 100 most-often-asked housecleaning questions—from how to clean fireplaces to how to get those hard-water spots off shower walls. 183 pages, $6.95, paperback

---

USE THIS COUPON TO ORDER DON ASLETT'S OTHER BOOKS TODAY!

USE THIS COUPON TO ORDER DON ASLETT'S OTHER BOOKS TODAY!

USE THIS COUPON TO SEND FOR FREE INFORMATION FROM DON ASLETT!

USE THIS COUPON TO SEND FOR FREE INFORMATION FROM DON ASLETT!